Glimpses of Times Past
Glasgow and Lanarkshire

Acrylic Paintings
by
'glesca artist' - William M. Neilly

ISBN:-10:1480237612
ISBN-13:978-1480237612

Dedicated with love to my mother Elizabeth Smith Murray (ms McGilvray) who died age 19 years

and with love and eternal thanks to my parents John and Flora McNiven Neilly (ms Green)

ACKNOWLEDGMENTS

I would like to thank everyone who has helped, supported and encouraged me with the publication of this book, particularly my wife Sandra and our daughter Vivienne.

A special thanks to William E. McArthur, creator, owner and webmaister of **GlescaPals.com** – a social history website for families and pals all over the world to share memories and photographs of Glasgow, especially its East End and Bridgeton - for permission to use photographs as reference for some of my paintings and for designing and maintaining my web pages.

Selected Bibliography

Jenkins, Martin and Stewart, Ian (2010): *Bygone Glasgow,* Ian Allan Publishing Ltd., Surrey.
Eunson, Eric (1997): *Old Bridgeton and Calton,* Stenlake Publishing Ltd., Catrine, Ayrshire.
Adams, Gordon (1990): *A History of Bridgeton & Dalmarnock,* Hill & Hay Ltd., Glasgow.

INTRODUCTION

During the 1950s a wide ranging comprehensive development programme was initiated by the Corporation of the City of Glasgow. The aim of the programme was to clear almost 100,000 dwellings and relocate 60% of the affected population elsewhere. Twenty-nine districts within the city were targeted for demolition and renewal. The designated Comprehensive Development Areas included Bridgeton and Dalmarnock in the East End of Glasgow. However, the demolition of tenements and buildings in the area outpaced the construction of new buildings. By 1974 the city population had been reduced by more than a quarter to 816,000 and large areas of dereliction remained in Bridgeton and Dalmarnock.

Glasgow Eastern Area Renewal project (GEAR) was set up in 1976 to tackle the problem of economic decline in the East End. Between 1976 and 1985 GEAR had modernised some properties and had created some new housing. Additional jobs had been created and by 1987 the Scottish Development Agency had provided industrial units to attract industry. However despite these efforts tens of thousands of jobs were lost and large areas of Bridgeton and Dalmarnock were demolished in the process. Derelict and vacant land remained between the redeveloped areas for the next two decades.

Clyde Gateway is the name given to an area covering a large part of the East End of Glasgow, including Bridgeton, Dalmarnock and Parkhead, as well as Rutherglen and Shawfield in South Lanarkshire. The Clyde Gateway Urban Regeneration Company was established in 2007 as a partnership between Glasgow City Council, South Lanarkshire Council, Scottish Enterprise, with funding from the Scottish Government. It was recognised that Dalmarnock had suffered the most physical decline in the Clyde Gateway area over the past 40 years with its large pockets of vacant and derelict land. Clyde Gateway's Master Plan for Dalmarnock will, in addition to solving long-standing technical and infrastructure issues, create over the next two decades, up until 2028, a new neighbourhood comprising residential, business, industrial, commercial, transport and civic amenities, increasing the population of the area by 20,000.

The Glasgow 2014 Commonwealth Games and the construction of the Athletes' Village at Dalmarnock, in the heart of one of the UK's largest regeneration areas, saw further demolition of tenements and buildings. The Athletes' Village will however be transformed into a new residential community on completion of the games.

In this collection of paintings the author has tried to capture everyday life as it was when he was a child growing up in Bridgeton and Dalmarnock and the surrounding area. The paintings are supported by snippets of local history. Apart from the occasional painting most of the scenes are from the 1950s and 1960s. The collection of paintings is primarily intended for all those many thousands of people who lived and worked in the area or were relocated during the long period of economic decline. It is hoped that, for them, fond memories will come flooding back. For others, the paintings will give a glimpse of the past in the area of the Athletes' Village of the Glasgow 2014 Commonwealth Games, and in the place where they will make their home and place of work following the widespread improvements through the Clyde Gateway Urban Regeneration Project.

Bridgeton Cross Umbrella and Olympia Building following complete restoration under the auspices of the Clyde Gateway Urban Regeneration Project. The Grade A listed Bridgeton Cross Umbrella is the most instantly recognisable structure to be found in the Clyde Gateway area. Located at the junction of London Road, Orr Street, Olympia Street, James Street, Main Street and Dalmarnock Road, this famous and historic landmark was restored to its full glory in 2011. The imposing, Grade B listed, Olympia building on the gushet between Orr Street and Olympia Street and facing Bridgeton Cross was completely revamped and returned to public use in 2012. The four-storey, Grade B listed, tenement at the junction of London Road and Orr Street flanks the former Bridgeton Central Railway Station.

Prints of any of the original acrylic paintings featured in this book can be obtained from the author's website:

www.glescapals.com/profiles/wneilly.htm

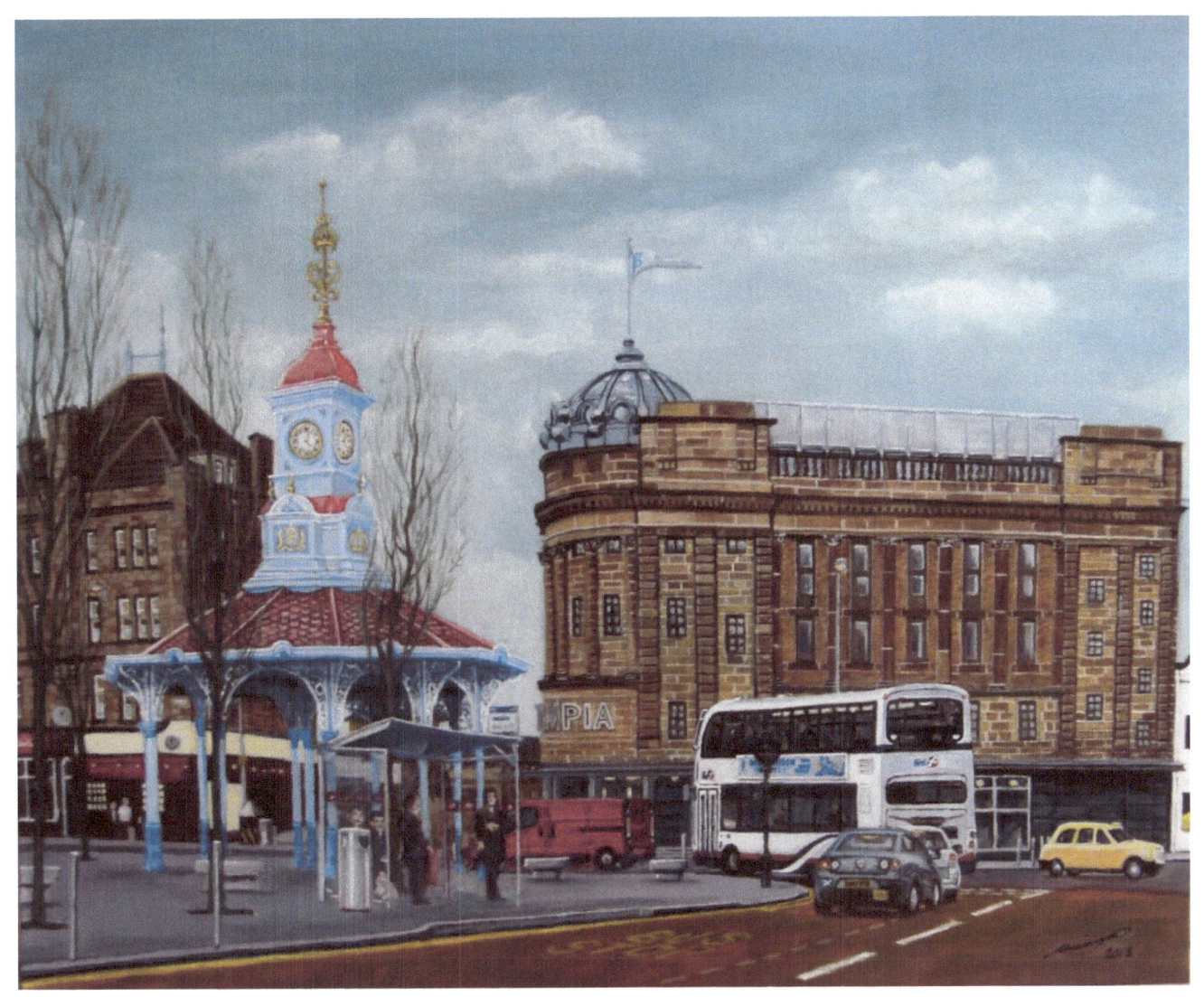

BRIDGETON UMBRELLA AND OLYMPIA BUILDING - © MARCH 2013
Acrylic on canvas board measuring 508 x 406 mm (20" x 16")

GLASGOW

In the 6th century when Saint Mungo founded a religious settlement Glasgow was a small fishing village located adjacent to the shallow and easily forded River Clyde. The village expanded through the centuries and in the early days Glasgow Cross, known as Mercat (Market) Cross after the market that was held there, grew in commercial importance and soon became recognized as the town centre. Glasgow Cross is formed by High Street to the north, Saltmarket to the south, Gallowgate and London Road to the east, and Trongate to the west. Glasgow was not a walled city and "gate" as in for example, Gallowgate, means "the way to" the gallows.

The industrial revolution took hold of Glasgow at the beginning of the 1800s. The manufacture of cotton, textiles, chemicals, glass, paper and soap increased rapidly with the cotton industry alone employing almost a third of the city's workforce at its height. The city diversified into heavy industries like shipbuilding, locomotive construction and other heavy engineering that could thrive on nearby supplies of coal and iron ore. Glasgow's population of 275,000 in 1841 made it twice the size of Scotland's capital city, Edinburgh.

In 1894 when Glasgow Corporation exercised its right to take over the running of the tramcar system, from the private operators, the trams were carrying 54 million passengers a year and were being drawn by 3,500 horses. Electrification was introduced in 1898 and by 1902 the horse-drawn trams were phased out. Coronation tramcars, with their distinctive domed roof, were introduced in 1937 and in 1949 Glasgow Corporation introduced trolley buses to replace some of the city's tram services. Motor buses, which had been introduced as early as 1914, became popular as the suburbs grew. They were more flexible than tramcars and trolley buses which were confined to main roads carrying overhead electric power wires. The last tram route to survive was service number 9 (Dalmuir West and Auchenshuggle) and this was withdrawn on 4 September 1962. Trolley buses which were unloved by Glaswegians were withdrawn in 1967.

A Foggy Evening at Glasgow Cross is typical of Glasgow Cross in the 1950s. The conductor of service number 15, standard hex-dash tramcar, prepares to flip the bow as the tramcar reverses at the crossover at the junction of Gallowgate and London Road. Service number 15 will then travel eastwards along Gallowgate to Parkhead Cross. Tolbooth Steeple, built in 1626 and the last remnant of a former Town Hall and prison, is just visible towering above the standard hex-dash tramcar. The Coronation tramcar, service number 9, is travelling eastwards along London Road to Auchenshuggle via Bridgeton Cross. Glasgow Cross railway station, occupying the central island behind the Coronation tramcar, closed in 1964 along with the low level railway running beneath London Road and Argyle Street.   The Mercat building completed in 1928 is just discernible through the fog on the right behind the railway station. The façade of the Mercat building has two ionic columns and the impressive edifice provides drama and grandeur at this point of entry to Glasgow's East End.

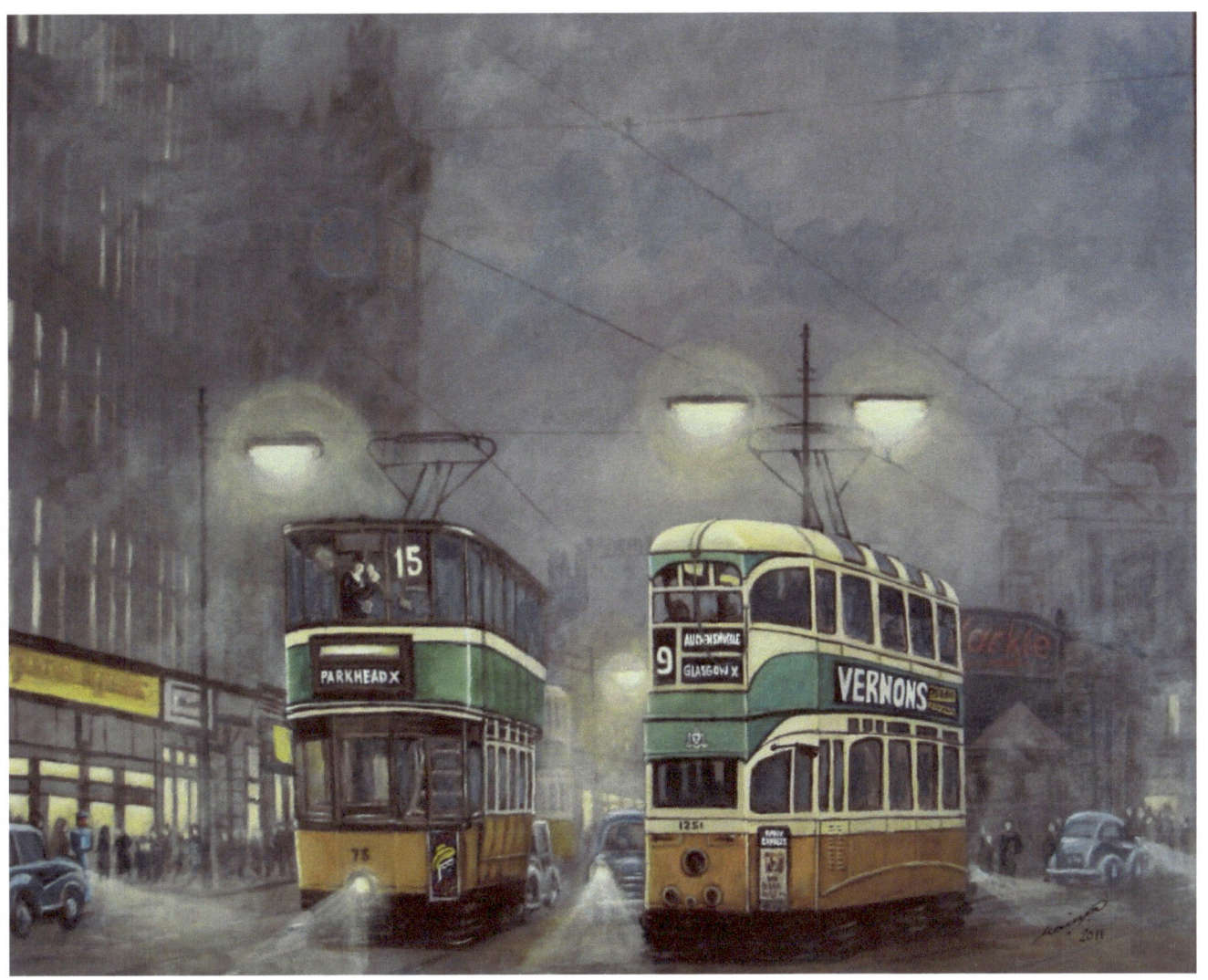

A FOGGY EVENING AT GLASGOW CROSS - © DECEMBER 2011
Acrylic on canvas board measuring 508 x 406 mm (20" x 16")

PARKHEAD CROSS

Parkhead Cross lies about 2 miles eastwards along the Gallowgate from Glasgow Cross. Parkhead Cross, originally the "Sheddens" – a general term used for a place where roads divide – is the centre of Parkhead. By 1794 the mining communities of Parkhead and neighbouring Westmuir had formed a village with a population of around 700. By the mid-19th century handloom weaving was extensively carried out in the weaving sheds situated on the ground floor of the one or two storey thatched houses. However handloom weaving had given way to heavy industry by the 1890s. The construction of William Beardmore's Parkhead Forge in 1837 attracted large scale migrants from England and Ireland into the area and soon the old weavers' houses around Parkhead Cross were replaced with four storey red sandstone tenements and impressive bank and other listed buildings. Though heavy engineering and steel were dominant, there was a wide variety of industries in the East End, such as rope walks, glass bottle, oil and chemical works, brickworks and potteries. Parkhead is the home of Scotland's "other national drink made wi' girders" – Barr's Irn Bru and of course Celtic Football Club which owns Celtic Park. Celtic Park, built in 1892 and completely upgraded and redeveloped in 1999, hosted the opening ceremony of the Glasgow 2014 Commonwealth Games. Being located adjacent to the Athletes' Village and with a seating capacity of 60,000 made Celtic Park an ideal venue for the opening ceremony.

Saturday Night at Parkhead Cross is an atmospheric and nostalgic scene typical of Parkhead Cross during the 1950's. Looking west along the Gallowgate, Burgher Street is immediately to the left of the two women returning home from a day's shopping. A tramcar emerges from Springfield Road in front of the green Morris Minor estate car. Two Coronation tramcars, built by Glasgow Corporation Tramways, make their way along the Gallowgate from the City Centre en route to Shettleston and Tollcross. Service number 1, en route to Scotstoun West from Dalmarnock is about to negotiate the tight curve into Duke Street from which emerges service number 30 en route to Dalmarnock from Blairdardie in the northwest of the city. The tight curve from Gallowgate into Duke Street prevented the use of modern bogie cars and services 1 and 30 were the last routes in the UK worked entirely by traditional four-wheel trams. This five-way, heavily used, tramway junction had to have the correct road for cars set by a points-man who was seated in the control tower shown behind the cream Morris Minor estate car. The estate car is travelling eastwards along Tollcross Road towards Mount Vernon and Uddingston. The pedal cyclist is turning into Westmuir Street leading to Shettleston.

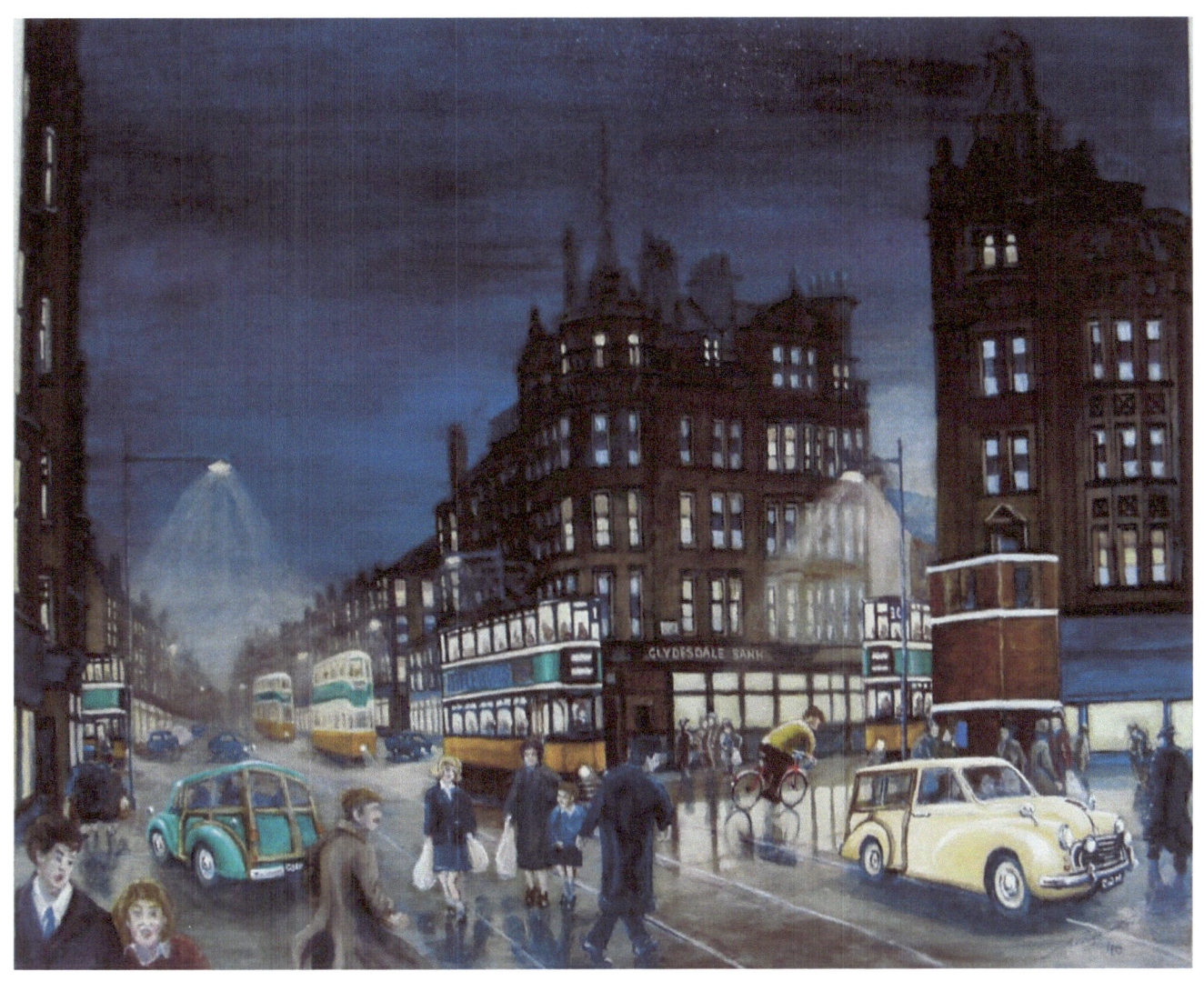

SATURDAY NIGHT AT PARKHEAD CROSS - © FEBRUARY 2010
Acrylic on canvas board measuring 508 x 406 mm (20" x 16")

PARKHEAD STADIUM RAILWAY STATION

Parkhead railway station opened in the late 1890s and served the East End of Glasgow on the Bridgeton and Carmyle Junction. The station was located in a cutting between Dalmarnock Street (later renamed Springfield Road) and Helenvale Street. It was later overlooked by what is now Whitby Street but which was then known as Winston Street in honour of Sir Winston Churchill. The railway was in tunnel along the length of London Road emerging at Bridgeton Cross Station before joining the Glasgow Central Line, also in tunnel.

In July 1914 King George V, Queen Mary and their entourage disembarked at Parkhead railway station for a visit to Beardmore's Parkhead Forge, Rolling Mills and Steel Works. Because of its proximity to Celtic Park football ground the station was renamed Parkhead Stadium Railway Station on 3 March 1952. It was a victim of Beeching's "axe" to reform the railways and it closed in the late 1960s. The cutting was filled in and landscaped over in 1989.

Parkhead Stadium Railway Station shows how the railway station looked in 1963. My painting used as reference a GlescaPals.com black and white photograph that was also published in the Glasgow *Evening Times.* A passenger steam train en route to Carmyle from Bridgeton stands at the platform. The red sandstone tenements of Springfield Road at the junction of Janefield Street are in the background and the tenements of Whitby Street junction with Springfield Road are on the right overlooking the densely landscaped station. The floodlights of Celtic Park can be seen in the skyline. Buildings associated with Springfield steel foundry are on the left of the painting.

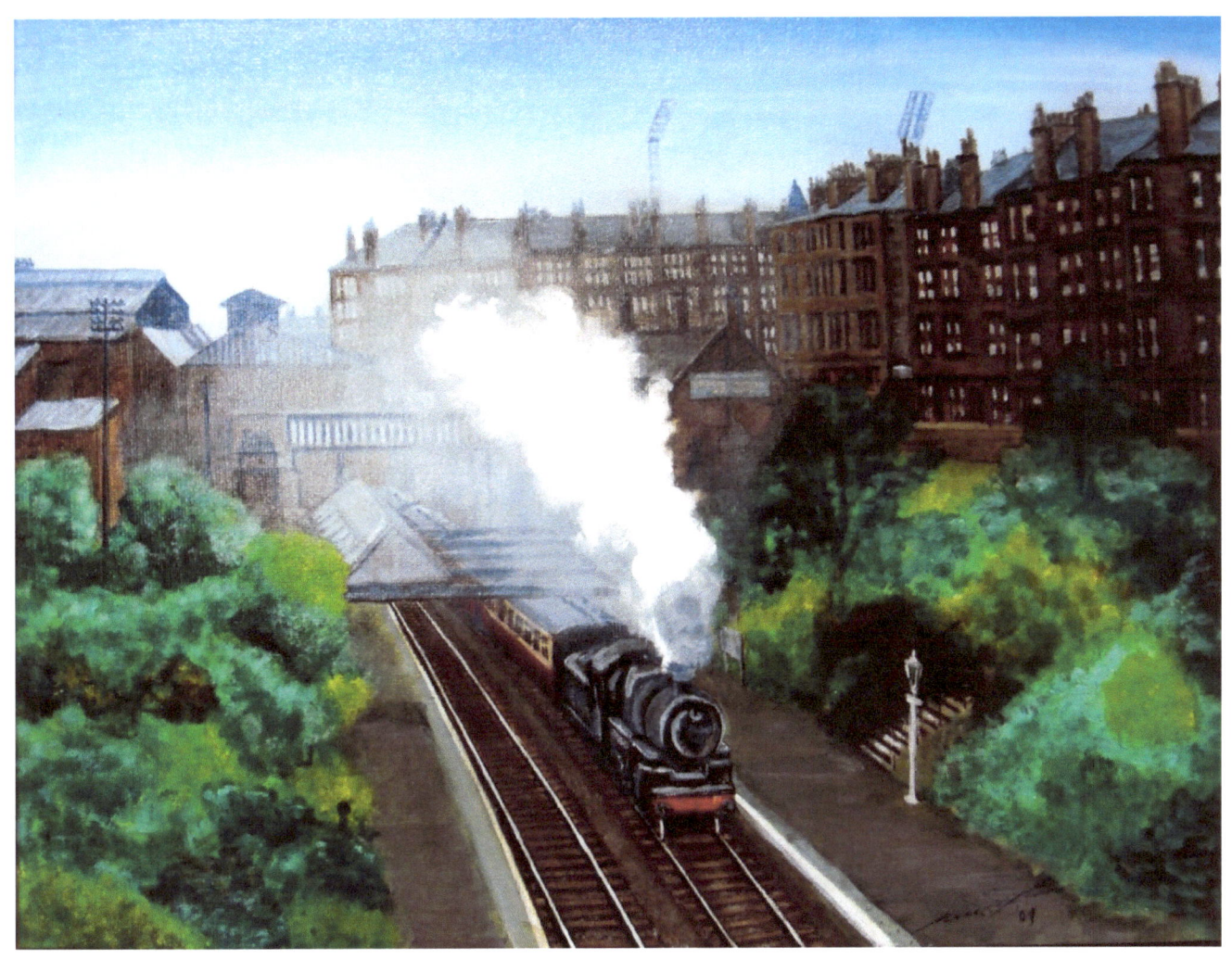

PARKHEAD STADIUM RAILWAY STATION - © JULY 2009
Acrylic on canvas board measuring 406 x 305 mm (16" x 12")

BRIDGETON

Bridgeton (pronounced Brig'ton by locals) is located less than one mile from Glasgow Cross to the south east of the City Centre. It is bounded by Glasgow Green to the west, Dalmarnock to the east and south and Calton to the north west.   In 1705 a portion of the Barrowfield estate was marked out for rent, by the third John Walkinshaw, and soon a small weaving village known as Barrowfield was established.   The village Main Street extended southwards to the River Clyde where in 1775 Rutherglen Bridge was constructed.   Barrowfield Tollhouse was built, at what is now known as Bridgeton Cross, to collect dues from users of the new bridge and the village developed from the "Toll" along Main Street to Rutherglen Bridge.   The 1795 Ordnance Survey map by Thomas Richardson shows the embryonic village of Barrowfield with the new Rutherglen Bridge and further upstream Dalmarnock Ford.   By 1816 the rapidly developing village of Barrowfield had been renamed Bridge Town and the boundary between Bridge Town and the mainly agricultural land of Dalmarnock was delineated by a burn flowing between what is now Dunn Street and Nuneaton Street. The burn crossed Dalmarnock Road and flowed along what is now known as Bartholomew Street and continued down Carstairs Street before outfalling to the River Clyde.   In 1847 Bridgeton along with Dalmarnock became part of the City of Glasgow and the East End became the manufacturing and industrial heart of Glasgow.

Built in 1875 the Grade A listed cast-iron shelter, known affectionately as the "Umbrella," occupies the centre of Bridgeton Cross.   It has always been, and still is, a popular meeting place for locals.   This famous and historic landmark was restored to its full glory in 2011 as part of the Clyde Gateway project with the Glasgow City Heritage Trust contributing to the cost of its refurbishment.   Towering over the "Umbrella" is the imposing façade of the Olympia Grade B listed building at the corner of Orr Street. Opened in 1911 as a variety theatre, it became the Olympia ABC cinema in 1924 and operated as such until its closure in 1974.   Following a period as a bingo hall and as a furniture store the building lay unused and derelict from the mid-1990s. The building suffered considerable internal damage by fire in 2004. It was purchased and brought back into public use by the Clyde Gateway project in 2012.

Saturday Night at Bridgeton Cross is an atmospheric and nostalgic scene typical of Bridgeton Cross on a Saturday night during the 1950s. Looking north, London Road is to the left and right of service number 26 tramcar en route to Burnside from Partick.   Orr Street is located behind the tramcar from which a taxi emerges behind the pedal cyclist. Pedestrians and traffic deal with rainy conditions as a news vendor sells newspapers at the "Umbrella".   *His Majesty O'Keefe,* starring Burt Lancaster and Joan Rice is showing in glorious Technicolor at the Olympia ABC cinema.

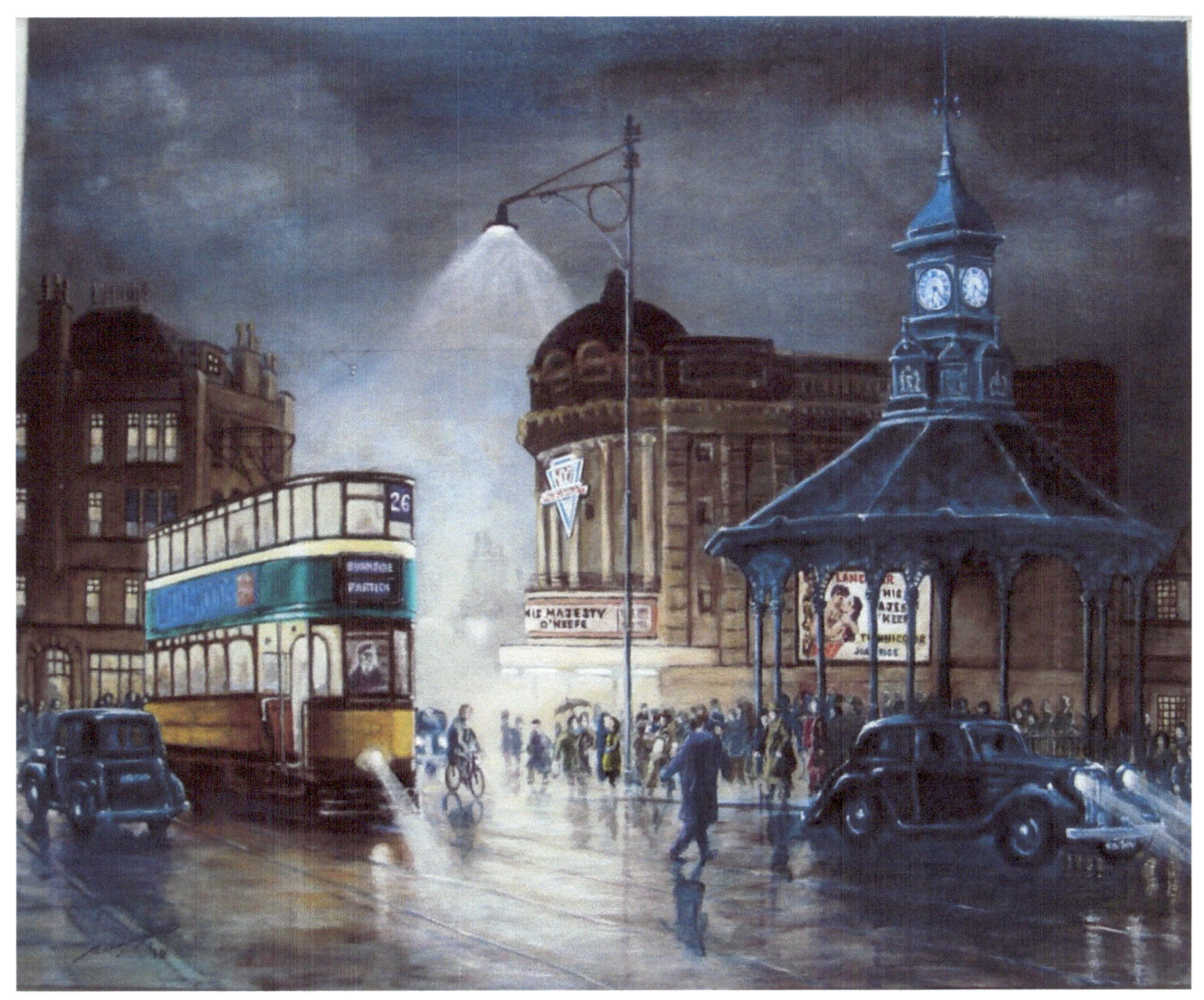

SATURDAY NIGHT AT BRIDGETON CROSS - © JANUARY 2010
Acrylic on canvas board measuring 508 x 406 mm (20" x 16")

BRIDGETON CROSS MANSIONS

Slum clearance of Barrowfield Toll in the early 1870s by the City Improvement Trust created the Bridgeton Cross shown in my paintings. The earlier one or two-storey, over crowded, properties with pitched, slated or tiled, roofs were replaced with red and yellow sandstone, four-storey, slate roof tenements erected around the new cross with the "Umbrella" being the focal point.   The Grade C listed, Georgian style, four-storey tenement on the left, designed by James Thomson a leading architect of the city's tenements, was built in 1871. The tenement curves into Dalmarnock Road and the curved corner has "Bridgeton Cross" inscribed on the parapet. The tenement opposite abuts the Grade B listed building erected in 1876 to the design of John Burnet, a renowned Glasgow architect. Burnet's building is an impressive blonde sandstone building of French influence with a bay window set within a large arched panel. This building abuts John Gordon's finely detailed bank building at the corner of Landressy Street. Bridgeton Cross Mansions with its onion-crowned turret was the last tenement to be built at the Cross in 1899. This Grade C listed, four-storey red sandstone tenement was designed by John Cunningham in 1896. Cunningham's design proved successful for gushet situations i.e. where the building stood on a corner with an acute angle between two roads, such as Dalmarnock Road and Main Street. His design was adapted for other tenements in the city, notably the gushet at Duke Street and Hunter Street, opposite John Knox Street.

Bridgeton Cross Mansions is typical of any weekday evening at Bridgeton Cross during the 1950s. Looking southwards beyond the "Umbrella", Dalmarnock Road is to the left from which service number 17 tramcar from Farme Cross enters Bridgeton Cross.   Two taxis emerge from Main Street to the right of service number 26 standard hex-dash tramcar en route from Burnside to Scotstoun via Partick. James Street is located immediately to the right of the two taxis.   The tramcar on the left, service number 26A, is en route to Shawfield via Main Street. The carter, in front of the "Umbrella", is heading towards the coal depot in Dalmarnock Road.

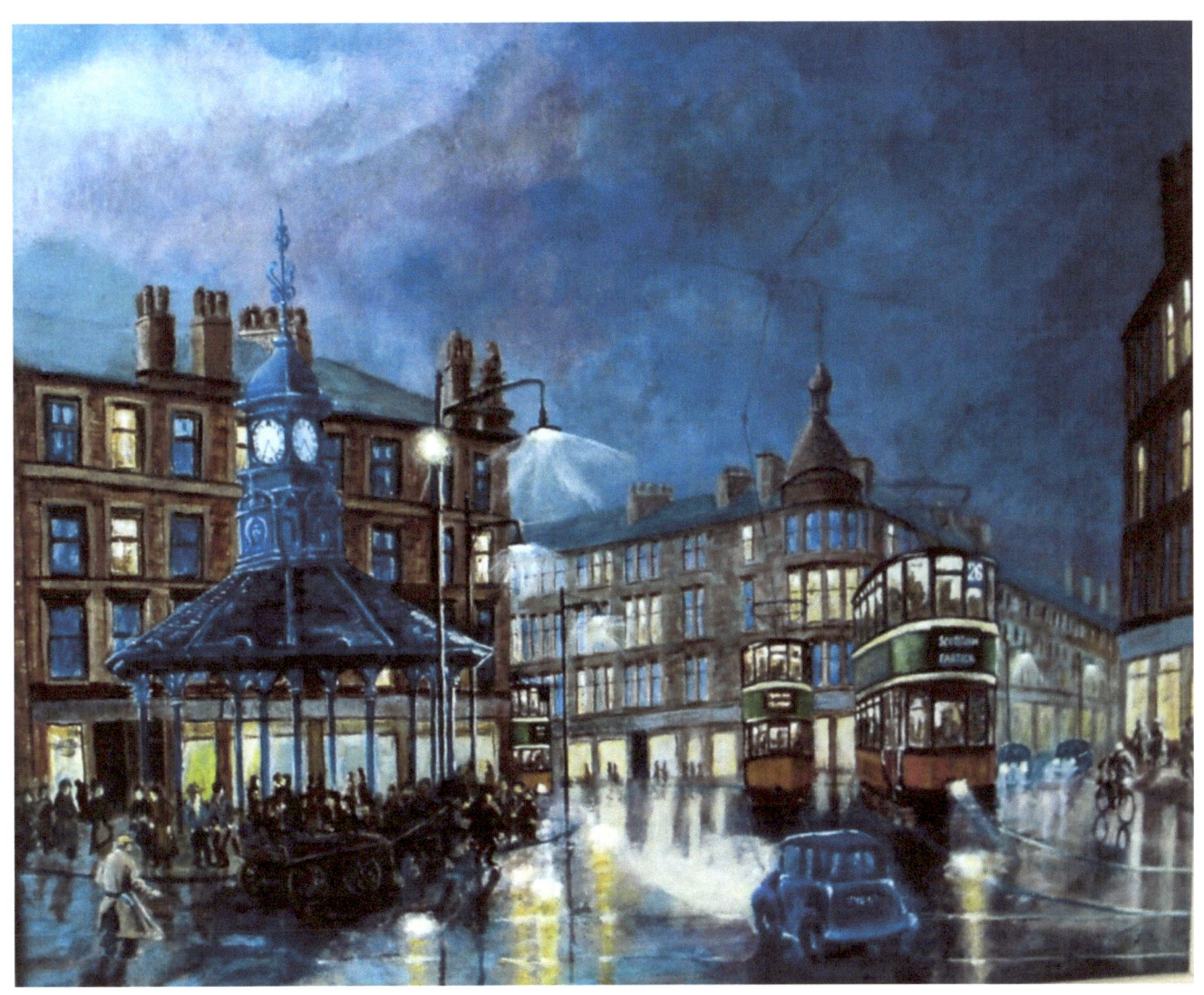

BRIDGETON CROSS MANSIONS - © MARCH 2007
Acrylic on canvas board measuring 508 x 406 mm (20" x 16")

BRIDGETON RAILWAY STATIONS

Bridgeton Central Railway Station was opened in 1872 by the North British Railway Company. The two-storey, seven arch frontage is flanked on both sides by four-storey, Grade B listed, tenements which were designed by Thomson and Turnbull in 1897 for the North British Railway Company. The railway lines from Bridgeton Central connected with the NBR Glasgow to Edinburgh line and also the NBR City and District line at Queen Street Station. There was also a connection with the Glasgow and South Western Railway at St Enoch Station (demolished 1977). Bridgeton Central was the terminus for the Balloch and Helensburgh services which ran on the City and District line. The London North Eastern Railway operated Bridgeton Central from 1923 until 1948 when nationalization made all railway companies British Rail. The station closed to passengers on 5 November 1979 but remained in use as a depot until 1 June 1987 when the station building was then converted to mixed commercial and residential use.

Bridgeton Cross Railway Station was opened in 1892 by the Caledonian Railway Company on its Glasgow Central line which is in tunnel beneath London Road, Glasgow Green, Glasgow Cross and Glasgow Central Station (Low Level). The lines from Bridgeton to Dalmarnock and Parkhead are also in tunnel. The London and Midland Scottish Railways operated Bridgeton Cross Station from the 1920s until nationalization. The station was a victim of Beeching's "axe" to reform the railways and it closed in 1964. A refurbished and renamed station, Bridgeton, re-opened in 1979 as part of Clyde Rail. It provides commuter services from Hamilton and Motherwell, via Dalmarnock Station, into Glasgow Central Station and beyond to the western suburbs. Plans to re-open the line between Bridgeton and Parkhead for the Glasgow 2014 Commonwealth Games never materialized.

Bridgeton Central Railway Station shows Glasgow Corporation Transport vehicles, around 1960, filing past the railway station which is located in London Road immediately to the west of Bridgeton Cross. Electric trolley bus, service number 106, en route to Bellahouston from Riddrie/ Millerston, is turning into Bridgeton Cross. It is followed by service number 46 motor bus en route to Castlemilk from Cranhill. Coronation Mark I tramcar, service number 9, en route to Auchenshuggle from Dalmuir West is directly in front of the railway station. The station entrance is just visible to the right of the tram.

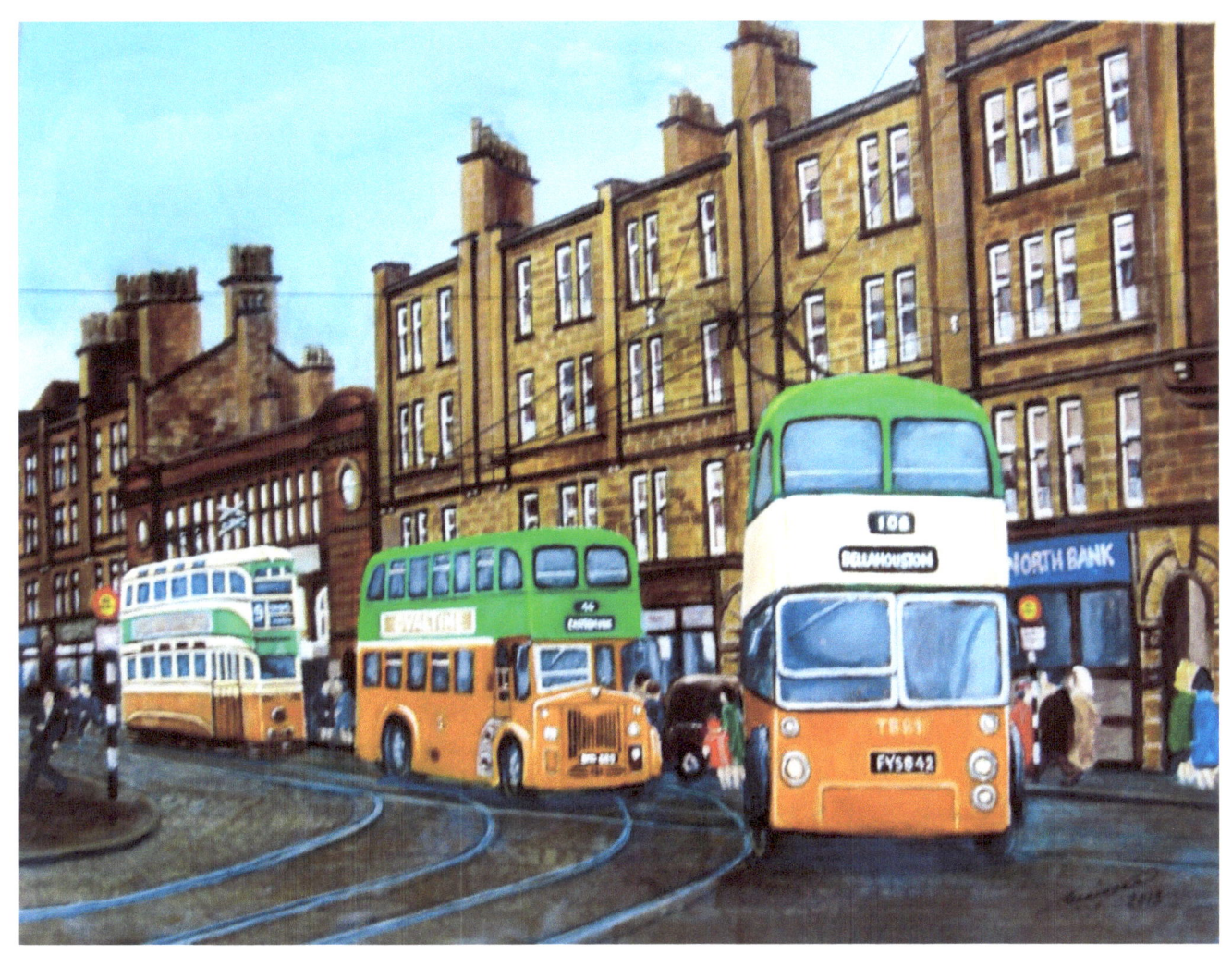

BRIDGETON CENTRAL RAILWAY STATION - © JANUARY 2013
Acrylic on canvas board measuring 406 x 305 mm (16" x 12")

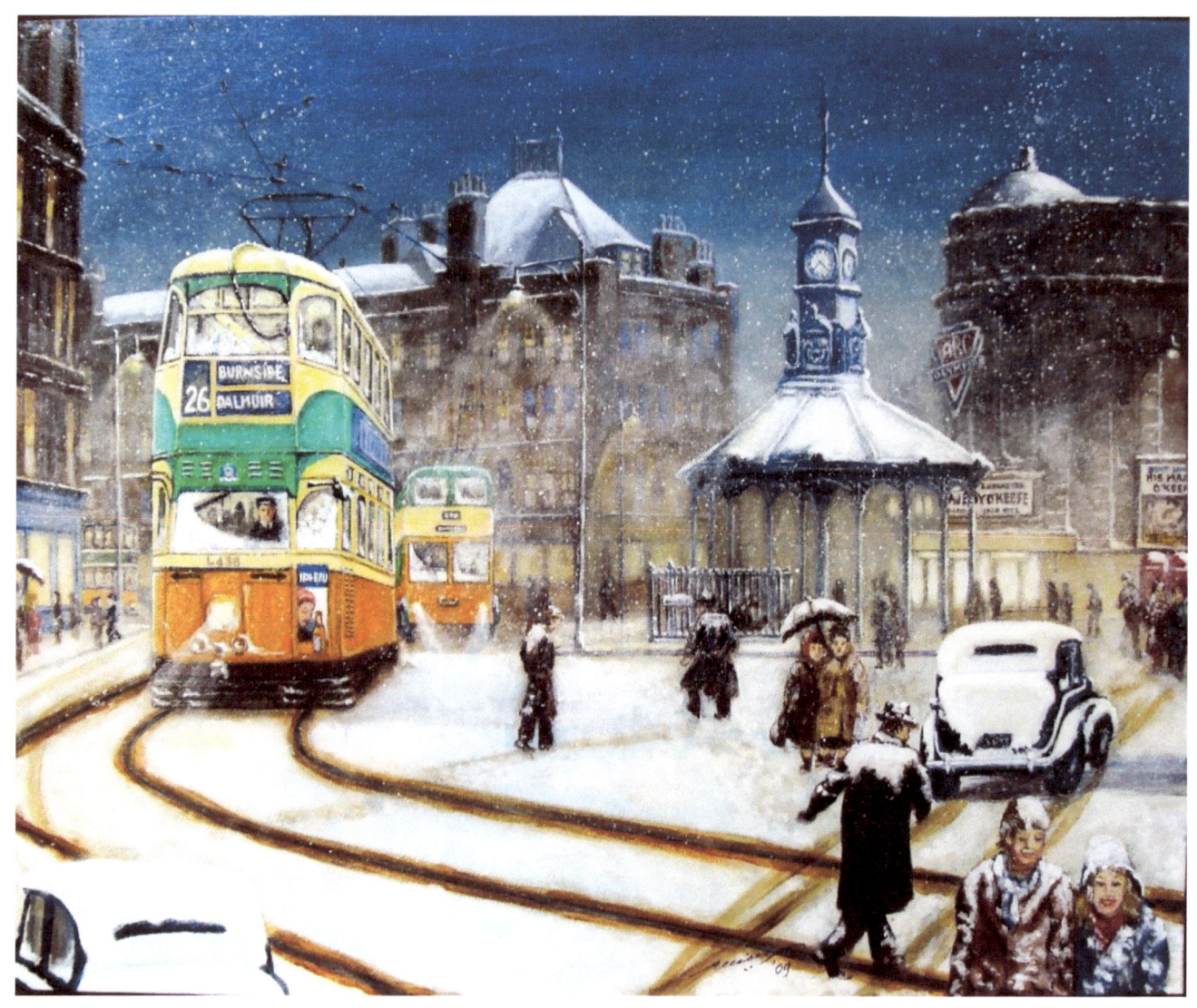

SNOWING AT BRIDGETON CROSS - © JANUARY 2009
Acrylic on canvas board measuring 508 x 406 mm (20" x 16")

Coronation Mark I, service number 26, tramcar en route to Burnside via Dalmarnock Road followed by electric trolleybus service number 106 en route to Bellahouston via James Street and Govan Cross.

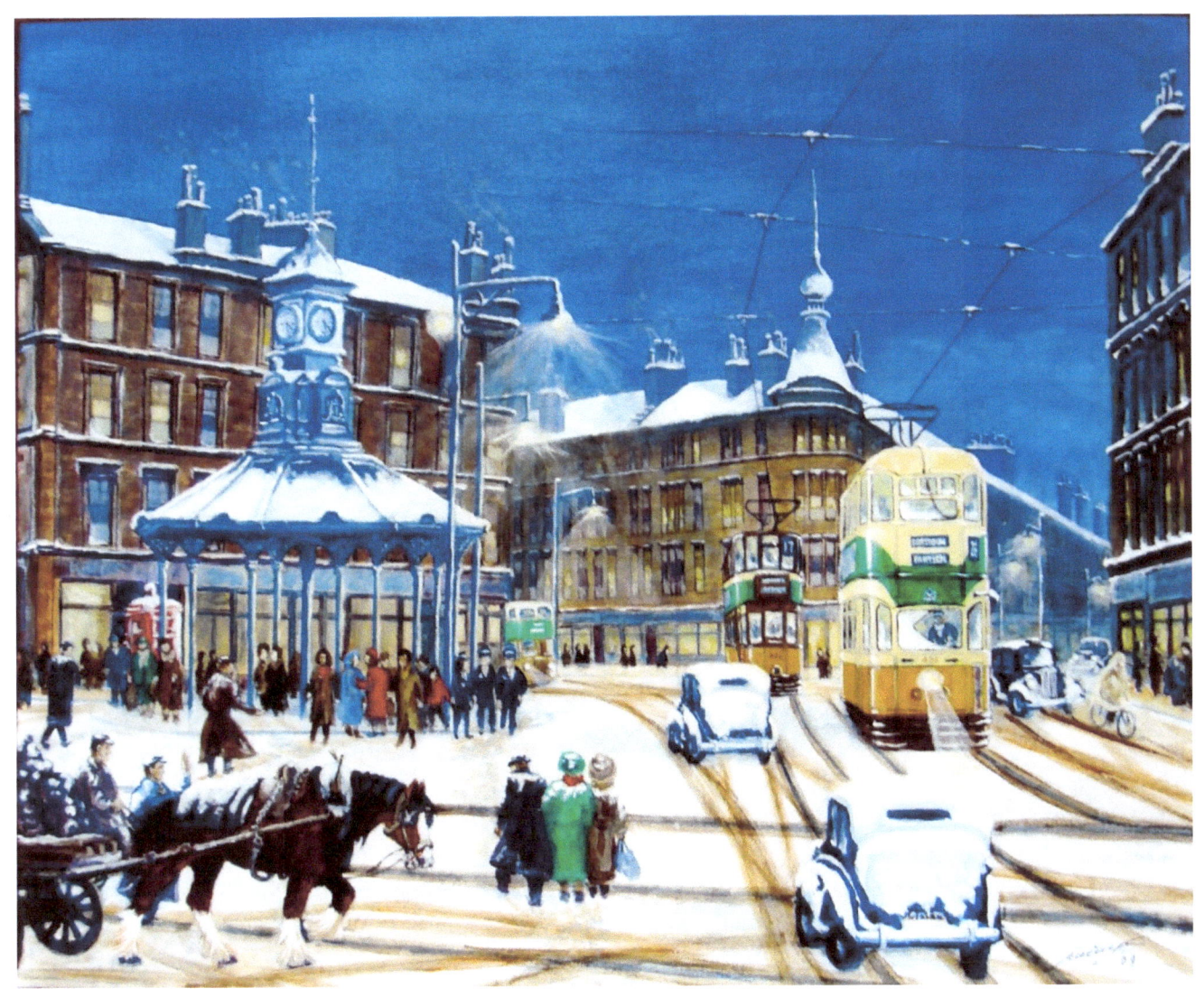

WINTER AT BRIDGETON CROSS - © FEBRUARY 2009

Acrylic on canvas board measuring 508 x 406 mm (20" x 16")

Coronation Mark II "Cunarder" tramcar city bound with service number 17, standard hex-dash, tramcar en route to Farme Cross via Dalmarnock Road.

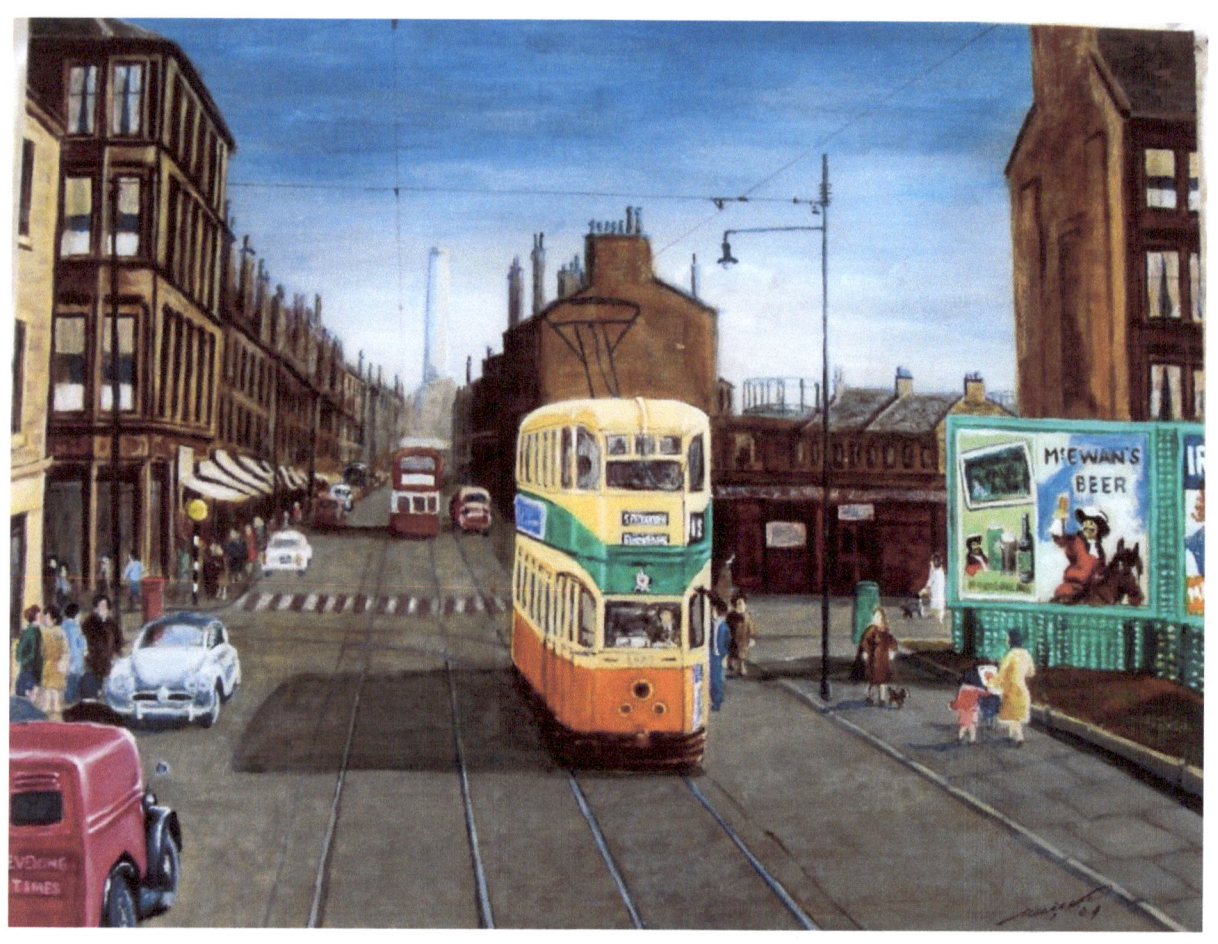

DALMARNOCK ROAD AT DALE STREET/ RUBY STREET - © FEBRUARY 2009
Acrylic on canvas board measuring 406 x 305 mm (16" x 12")

Coronation Mark II "Cunarder" heading north along Dalmarnock Road having just emerged from the tram depot in Ruby Street on the left. Dale Street is on the right behind the billboards. Dalmarnock Gas Works tank holder can be seen in the skyline between the buildings. The tall concrete chimney of Dalmarnock Power Station looms above the red Central SMT motor bus heading south towards Dalmarnock Bridge and the suburbs beyond. The iron railway bridge at Dalmarnock Railway Station is clearly visible in front of the bus.

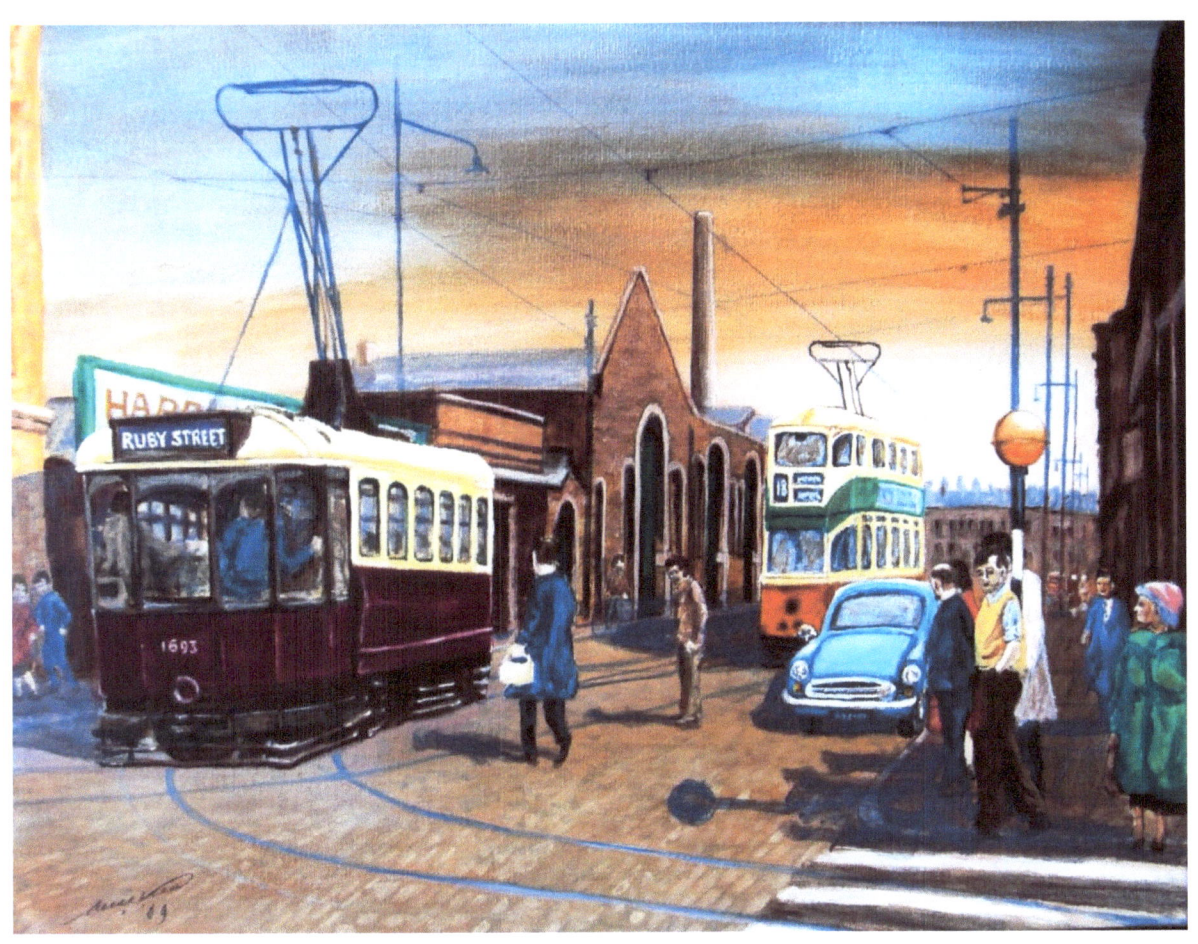

RUBY STREET TRAM DEPOT - © FEBRUARY 2009
Acrylic on canvas board measuring 406 x 305 mm (16" x 12")

Ruby Street tram depot was built in 1893 to accommodate over 300 horses for the city's horse-drawn trams. The depot was adapted for cars when the system was electrified mid-1901. The tram depot was demolished in 1967. A bogie, single deck, hex-dash car and a Coronation Mark I car are heading into the tram depot located on the left and opposite the "steamie" (public wash-house) flanked either side by red sandstone tenements.

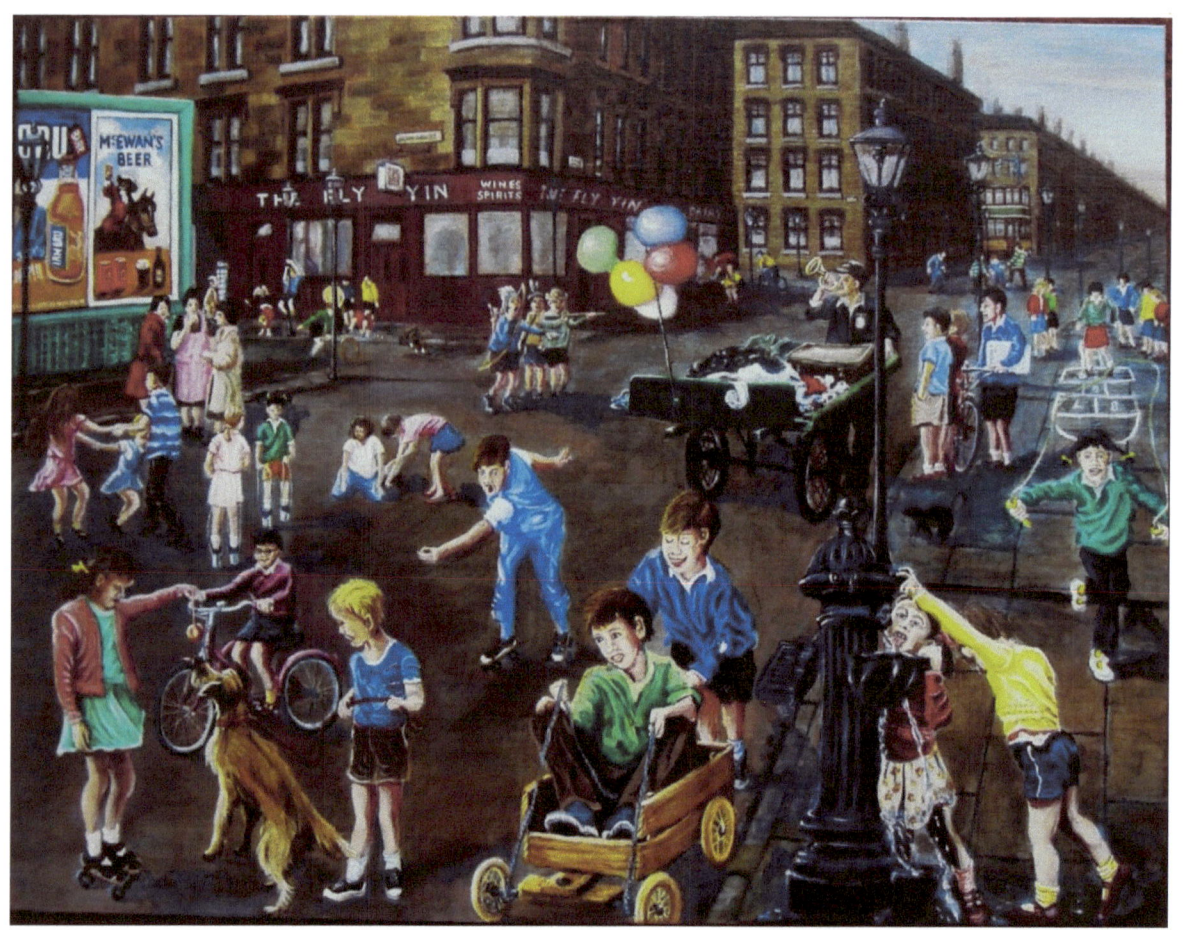

OOT TAE PLAY - © JANUARY 2009
Acrylic on canvas board measuring 508 x 406 mm (20" x 16")

When asked by their Ma or Da where they were going, as they headed towards the outside door of the house, the weans would often reply, "Oot tae play".   This meant playing with their pals in the backcourt or street with simple games such as: fitba'; roller skating; riding their bikes; go-carting (on homemade bogies made from an orange box and a set of old pram wheels or a pair of roller skates); walking on stilts (using tin cans); high heels (wearing your mothers favourite shoes); peever or beds (hopscotch); bools (marbles); skipping ropes; kick-the-can; climbing and dreepin' aff dykes, billboards or lamp posts; leap frog; hand stands; cowboys and indians; splashing about in puddles; tig; yo-yo, etc.

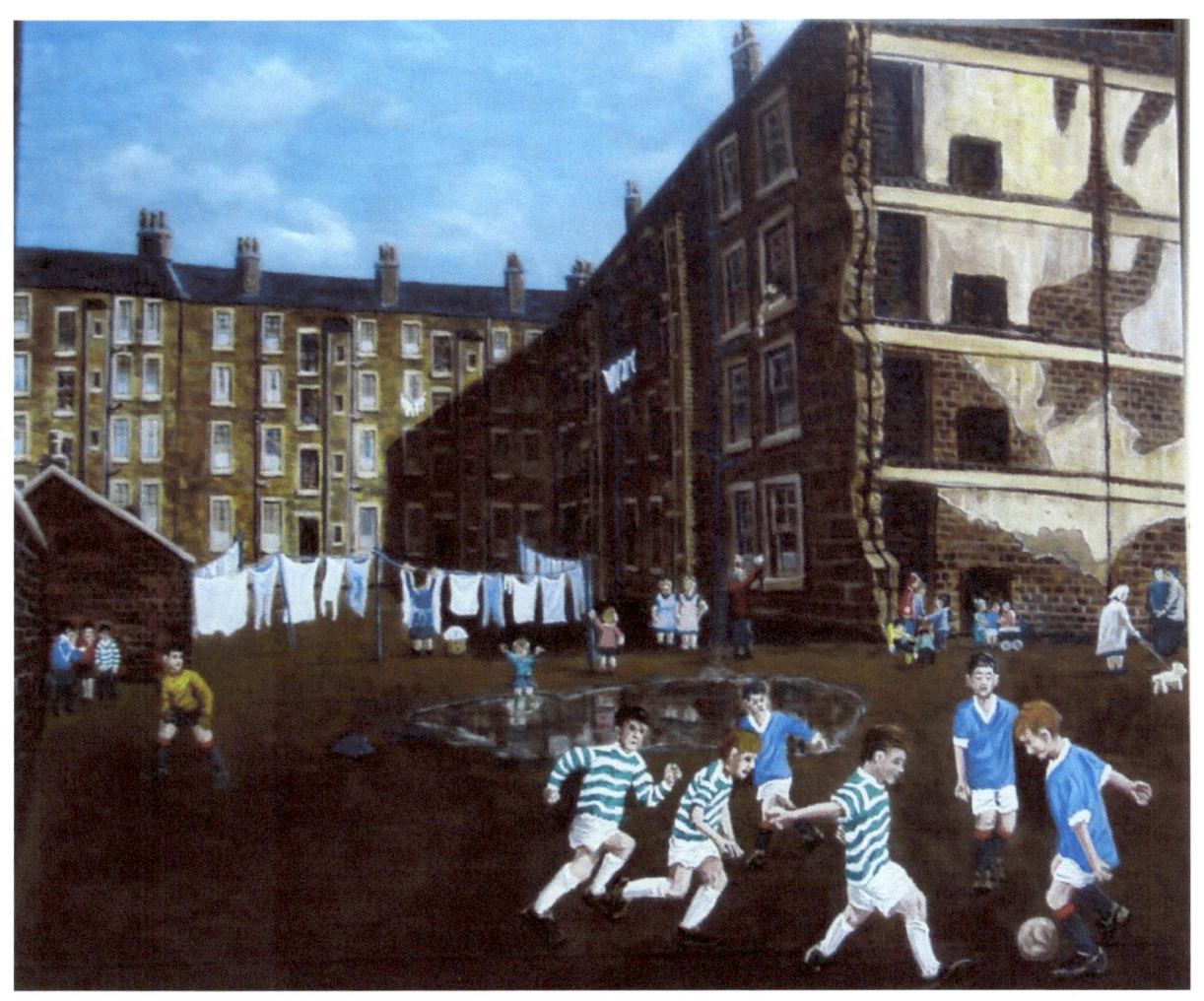

WASHDAY BLUES - © FEBRUARY 2011
Acrylic on canvas board measuring 508 x 406 mm (20" x 16")

The youngsters, in their Rangers and Celtic football strips, play in the backcourt of tenement houses which are in the process of being demolished due to re-development of the area. One woman is hanging out her washing having just taken her turn in the backcourt wash house. Two other women are having a blether and hoping that the dirty football doesn't hit their clean washing. A little girl enjoys playing in the puddle which is being created by waste water leaking from the tenement drain pipe.

Weans playing in the backcourt of their tenement making sandcastles from the sand and debris from partially demolished inter-connecting walls. Note that the weans are well wrapped up against the cold weather.

Images published in the *Evening Times – "Times Past"* supplement were used as reference for **Backcourt Sandcastles** and **Backcourt Weans.**

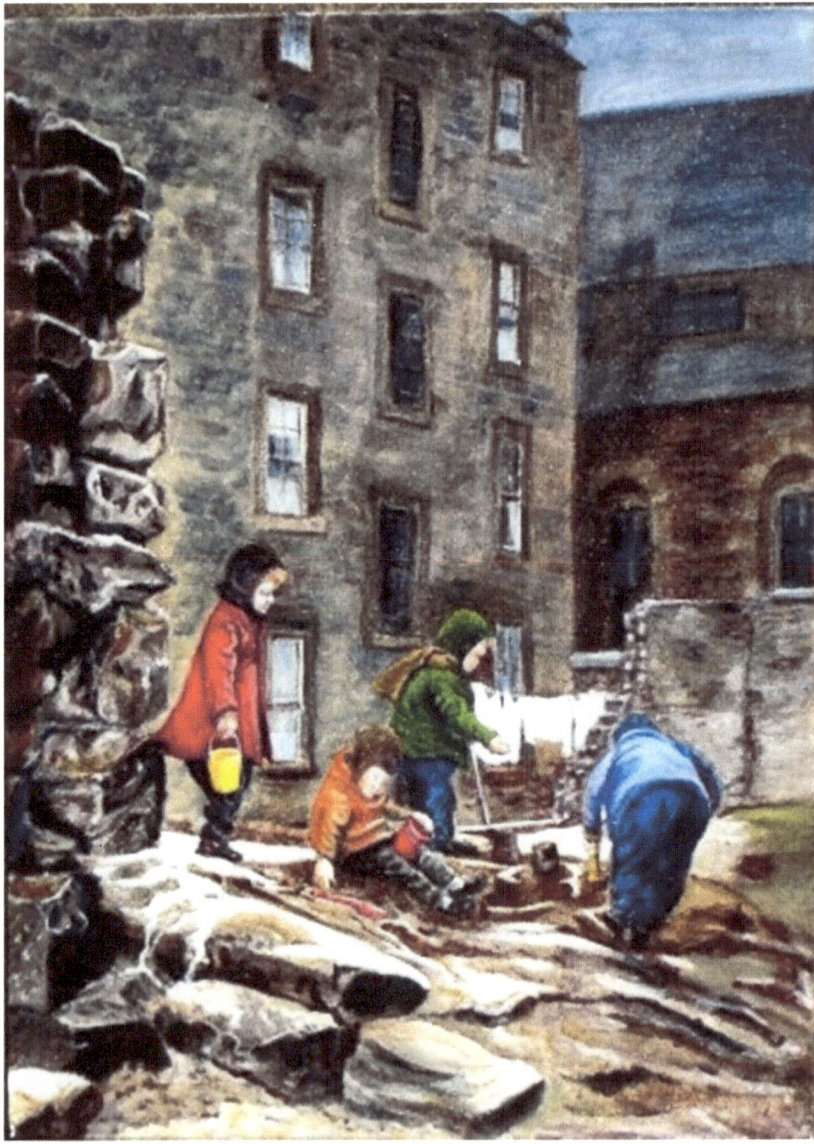

BACKCOURT SANDCASTLES - © APRIL 2007
Acrylic on canvas board measuring 406 x 305 mm (16" x 12")

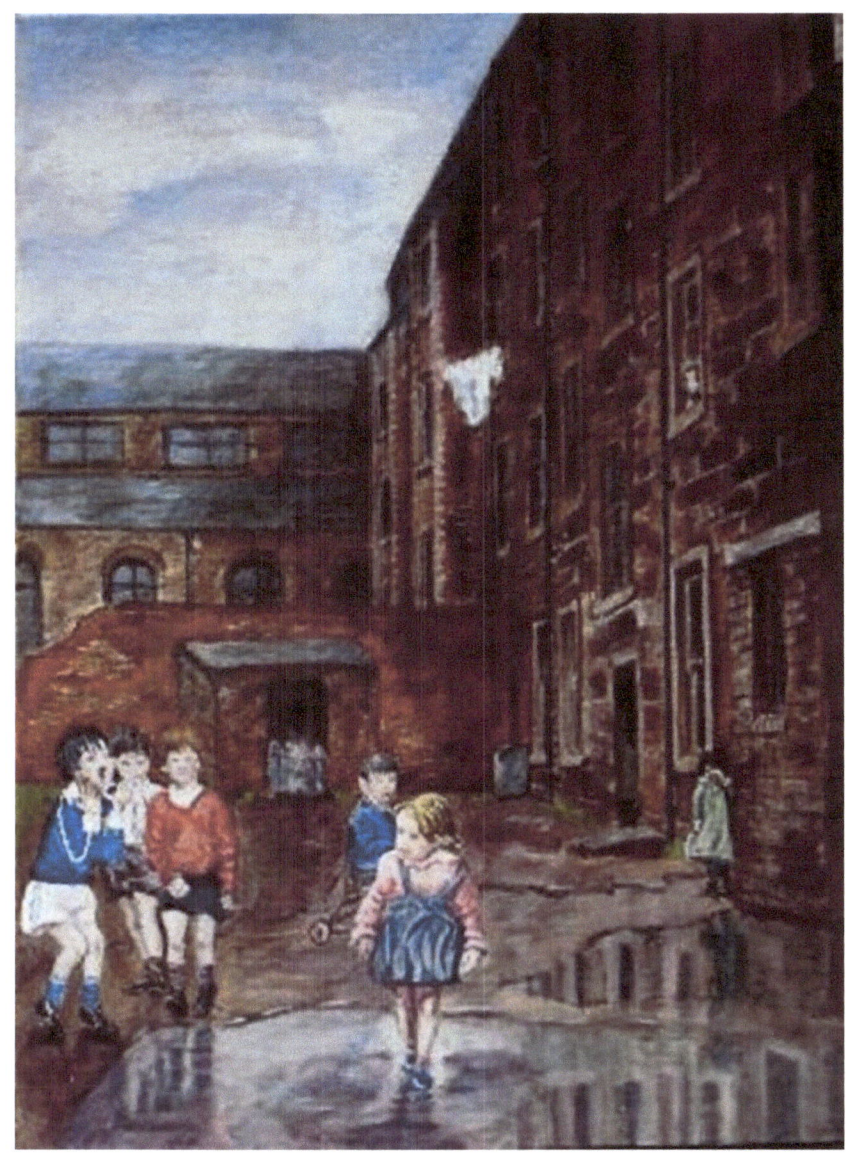

Weans playing in the backcourt of their tenement watched by a mother looking out the first storey window of her flat. The boy on the left shouts to his pals, "Do you want to join us for a game of fitba?" The wee lassie in the foreground splashes about in a stagnant puddle watched from behind by her brother on his tricycle. The wee girl crying is partially hidden by the outside lavatory that serves all the ground floor flats. The midden (trash) bins in the background obviously need emptying by the City Council.

BACKCOURT WEANS - © APRIL 2007
Acrylic on canvas board measuring 406 x 305 mm (16" x 12")

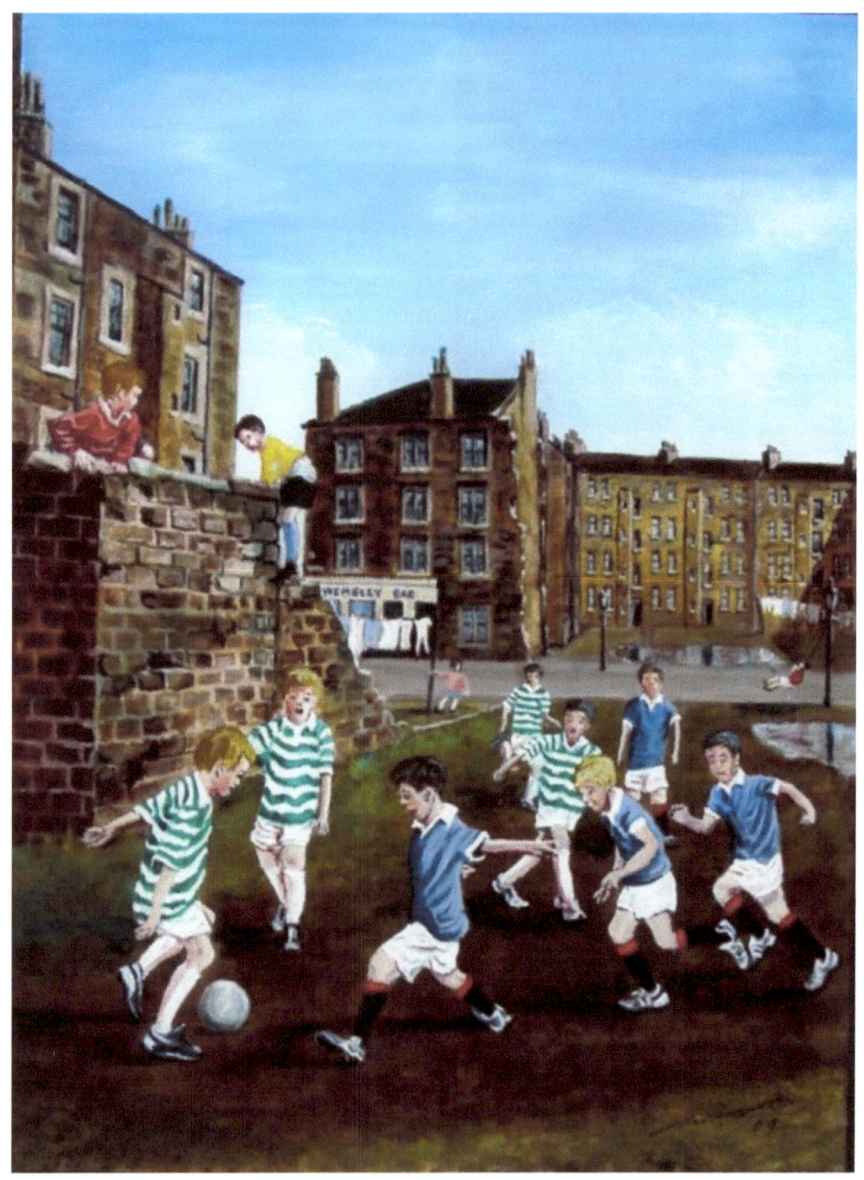

The Wembley Bar located at the junction of Dunn Street and Baltic Street in the East End of Glasgow was a favourite haunt of the locals. The tenements in Baltic Street are in the process of being demolished due to the re-development of the area. The background tenements front Dalmarnock Road between Dunn Street and Fairbairn Street. In the foreground some youngsters, dressed in their Rangers and Celtic strips, are kicking a ball about while two weans are climbing and dreepin' aff a dyke.

DREEPIN' AFF A DYKE - © APRIL 2007

Acrylic on canvas board measuring 406 x 305 mm (16" x 12")

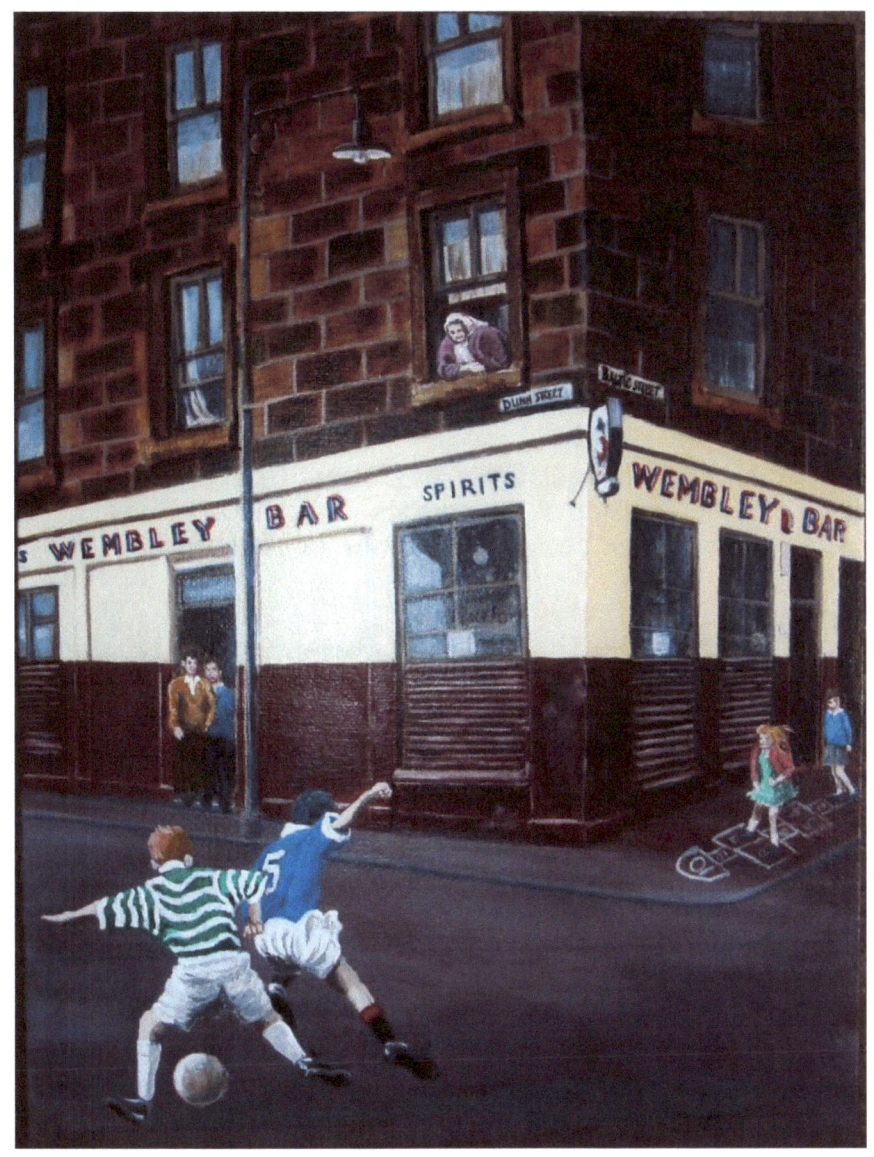

A close-up of the Wembley Bar at the corner of Dunn Street and Baltic Street in the East End of Glasgow. The Wembley Bar was owned by Benny McGowan and Benny's father "pop" cut a dash as he tended customers dressed in collar, tie, waistcoat and long white apron. The Wembley Bar and the surrounding tenements were demolished in the late 1960s and early 1970s. Two boys playing fitba' in their Rangers and Celtic strips are watched by two locals at the Dunn Street entrance to the pub while a woman is hingin' oot a windae above the pub. Two wee lassies are playing peever or "beds" in Baltic Street outside the other pub entrance and next to close number 206.

HINGIN' OOT A WINDAE - © APRIL 2007

Acrylic on canvas board measuring 406 x 305 mm (16" x 12")

DALMARNOCK

Dalmarnock is located in the south east of the city of Glasgow about two miles from Glasgow Cross. It lies on the north bank of the River Clyde between Bridgeton and Parkhead. Dalmarnock Bridge, where once there was a Ford, is the main route into Glasgow from Rutherglen and Hamilton. Bridgeton Cross is about one mile northwest from Dalmarnock Bridge along Dalmarnock Road and Parkhead Cross is located about one mile northeast of Dalmarnock Bridge along Springfield Road.

The name Dalmarnock is recorded in 1174 as "Dalmurnech" and derives from the Celtic words "Dael" and "Muranach", meaning the meadow or plain abounding in bent and iris. From a very early period the lands of Dalmarnock belonged to two families who were related to each other through marriage – Gray and Woddrop. The Grays owned Dalmarnock the Greater and the Woddrops, Dalmarnock the Lesser. These two families owned several other estates in and around Glasgow and William Allan Woddrop inherited from his father John, the estates of Dalmarnock, Elsrickle and Garvald. Maps of Scotland from the late 18th and early 19th century record the Woddrop mansion houses in Dalmarnock as belonging to "Wardrope" and "Waddrop".

Dalmarnock House was built in Dalmarnock the Greater and is shown along with several other mansion houses in the area on the 1773 map by Charles Ross. In 1784 John Gray sold Dalmarnock the Greater to his son-in-law, Thomas Buchanan and his son, John Buchanan, improved Dalmarnock House by renovating the frontage and by adding wings to the original mansion house. When Thomas Richardson published his map of Glasgow in 1795 a second Dalmarnock House had been built, in Dalmarnock the Lesser, by the Woddrop family. The two Dalmarnock Houses were located on either side of Dalmarnock Road immediately above Dalmarnock Ford less than 400 yards (375 metres) distant from each other. Their lodge houses stood opposite each other on Dalmarnock Road at Allan Street.

Dalmarnock at this time was still mainly agricultural land with coal, farm produce and cattle from Rutherglen and beyond still fording the River Clyde. Gordon Adams (1990) writes that the earliest history of Dalmarnock is associated with the strategic importance of the ford which had been in existence since Roman times. In medieval times it was probably used by the masons who helped build Glasgow Cathedral as they travelled to and from Rutherglen and Mary Queen of Scots is alleged to have used Dalmarnock Ford as she fled south following her defeat at the Battle of Langside in 1568.

The construction of a bridge at Dalmarnock in 1821 and the annexing of Dalmarnock by the City of Glasgow in 1847 saw the rapid development of industry and Dalmarnock becoming the city's powerhouse. Dalmarnock House on Dalmarnock the Greater was demolished around 1910 and the

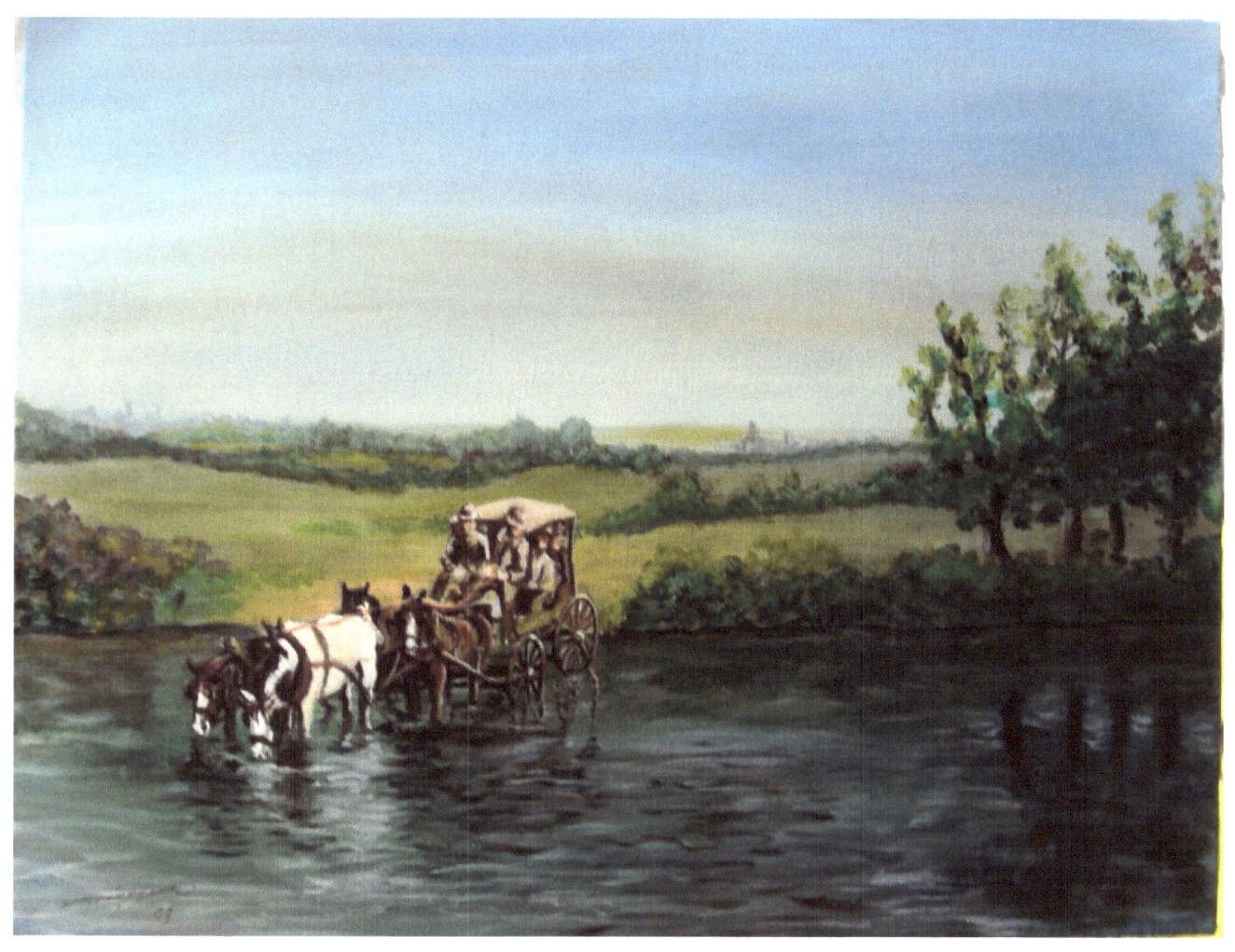

DALMARNOCK FORD - © OCTOBER 2009
Acrylic on canvas board measuring 406 x 305 mm (16" x 12")

How the ford may have looked in the early 19th century as a four-horse drawn carriage brings passengers across the river from Rutherglen. The river was so shallow at this point it was possible to wade across it. The construction of Glasgow Tidal Weir, in 1901 east of Albert Bridge, stabilised the upstream banking and created a deep, wide channel of water through Glasgow Green and beyond to Dalmarnock. Downstream of the weir is entirely tidal, alternating between fresh and sea water.

site cleared for the construction of an electric power station to satisfy the needs of industry, new housing, the electrified tramway network and the electric trolleybus services.

Dalmarnock House on Dalmarnock the Lesser survived until around 1937 when it was demolished to make way for "modern" grey sandstone, three-storey, tenements in Woddrop Street, Allan Street, Garvald Street and other surrounding streets. The former Dalmarnock Recreation Ground at the corner of Dunclutha Street and Ardenlea Street marked the spot of Dalmarnock House. The grey sandstone tenements comprised three and four apartment flats with kitchen and bathroom. The living room was heated by a coal fire with back boiler that provided hot water on tap. Each bedroom was heated with a gas fire and the kitchen had a gas-fired wash boiler, twin wash tubs and gas cooker. Communal grassed backcourts served as both washing drying greens and play areas and ground floor tenants also enjoyed their own front garden.

Prefabricated houses (prefabs) were erected in Dalmarnock the Lesser between 1944 and 1949 to provide urgently needed accommodation for citizens when World War II ended. The prefabs were a stop-gap until more permanent building could be started. They were delivered on a lorry and erected within hours on a concrete foundation. They were similar in style to a bungalow with front and large rear gardens with a shed to store coke (fuel for heating) and garden tools. The prefabs had a front, side and rear entrance and comprised two bedrooms with fitted wardrobes; living room with coke fired burner; bathroom with separate toilet (without wash hand basin); hot water on tap and a kitchen with the latest appliances such as twin wash tubs, wash boiler, cooker and refrigerator. The prefabs in Woddrop Street/ Dunclutha Street were a small part of the temporary housing which was concentrated between Allan Street/ Summerfield Street and Ardenlea Street.

Dalmarnock was designated as a Comprehensive Development Area in the 1960s. It was targeted for demolition and renewal. However the demolition of factories and tenements outpaced the construction of new buildings and large areas of vacant and derelict land remained with massive job losses. Glasgow Eastern Area Renewal (GEAR) project was set up to tackle the problem of economic decline and between 1976 and 1985 it modernised some properties and created some new housing. Gear Terrace off Allan Street commemorates this project. Clyde Gateway Urban Regeneration Company was established in 2007, a multi-agency, to physically transform the large pockets of vacant and derelict land at Dalmarnock into a new and thriving neighbourhood. Residential, business, industrial, commercial, transport and civic amenities will be created, increasing the population by 20,000 over the next two decades up until 2028. The Glasgow 2014 Commonwealth Games and the construction of the Athletes' Village at Dalmarnock saw further demolition of tenements and buildings. However, on completion of the games, the Athletes' Village will be transformed into a new residential community.

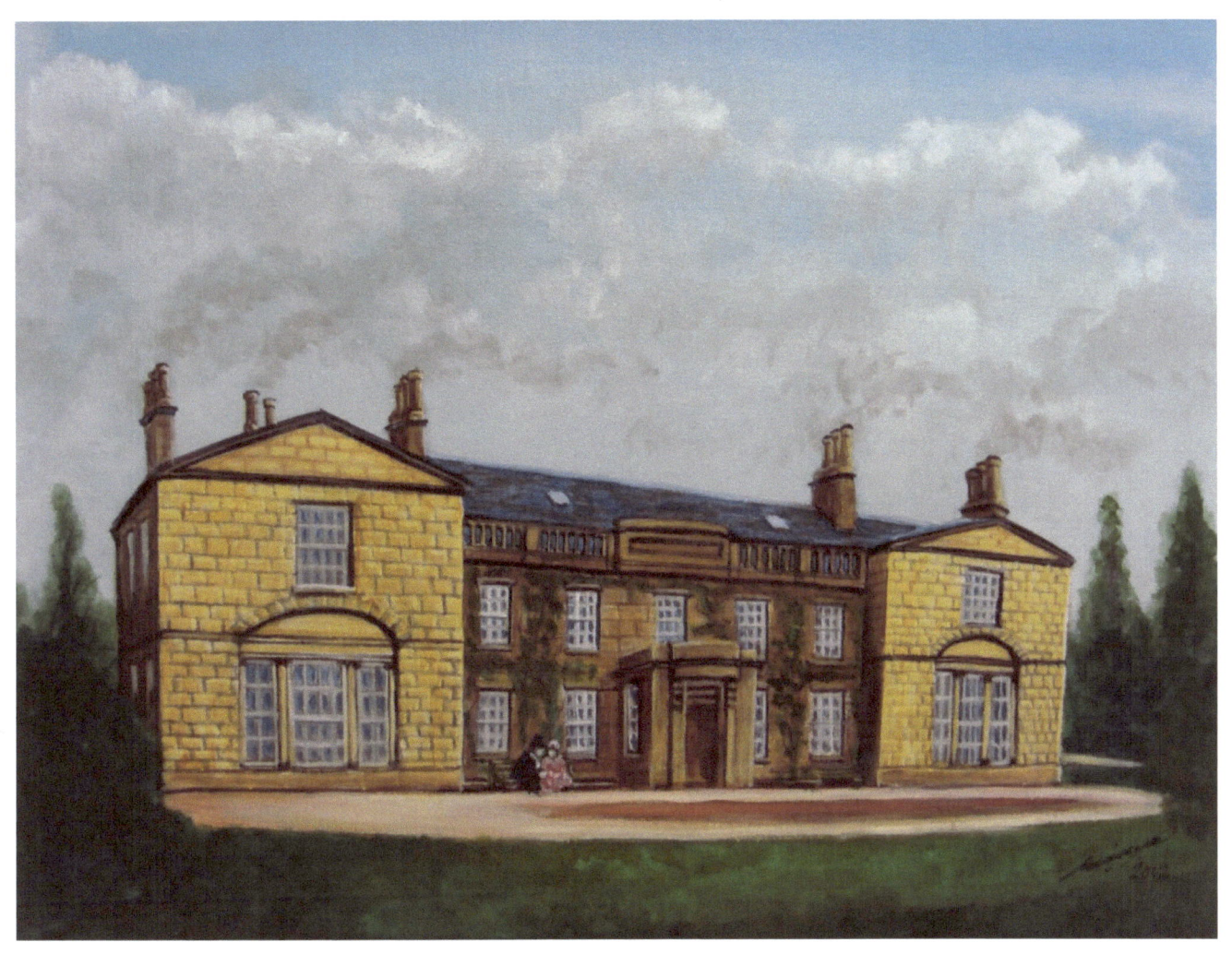

DALMARNOCK HOUSE 1870 - © NOVEMBER 2012
Acrylic on canvas board measuring 406 x 305 mm (16" x 12")

Dalmarnock House, built circa 1773, showing the new frontage and wings added to the original mansion house by John Buchanan of Ardoch. My painting used as reference a photograph taken in 1870 by Thomas Annan. Dalmarnock House was demolished around 1910 and the site cleared for the construction of Dalmarnock Electric Power Station in 1913.

DALMARNOCK BRIDGE

The first flat road bridge across the River Clyde in Glasgow was built in 1821 by the Road Trustees at Dalmarnock. The bridge comprising eight spans was constructed of timber and located adjacent to Dalmarnock Ford. It is the furthest up river of any of the city's bridges and it links Dalmarnock with the ancient Royal Burgh of Rutherglen on the south bank of the river. Coal from Farme Coal Pit in Downiebrae was transported across the bridge along with other goods and produce. The Road Trustees had power to levy tolls from carts, carriages, cattle and persons on foot using the bridge so they built Dalmarnock Tollhouse around 1820, at 556 Dalmarnock Road opposite Springfield Road, to collect the tolls.

A replacement eight span timber bridge of similar design was built in 1848 as the supporting timbers of the original bridge were founded on sand causing the bridge to become like a switchback as the timber supports gave way. This bridge was replaced with the present five span bridge built in 1891 and refurbished in 1997. The present bridge was also constructed close to the site of Dalmarnock Ford.

In 1913 Glasgow Corporation Electricity Department purchased the land occupied by Dalmarnock House, on Dalmarnock Greater estate, to build a 100,000 kilowatt coal-fired power station. The outbreak of World War I in 1914 halted the work and it was not until 1920 that the first electricity was generated. A second phase was completed in 1926 and the growing demand for electricity led to various additions and enlargements over the years, including the construction in 1955 of a new boiler house with its landmark concrete chimney. Dalmarnock Electric Power Station which survived bombing raids during World War II was closed in 1977 by the South of Scotland Electricity Board and flattened three years later. The site lay unused, vacant and derelict for more than two decades. Clyde Gateway's Master Plan for Dalmarnock will include a multi-million pound makeover of this historic riverbank site.

Dalmarnock Bridge 1827 was painted using as reference an image available from Glasgow University Library (MS Murray 636) which shows the bridge in 1827. The bridge is viewed from the south bank (Rutherglen) and looks upstream towards the meadow, used for cattle grazing, on the north bank and in the grounds of Dalmarnock Lesser estate where the Woddrop family's Dalmarnock House is located. The people on the rowing boat are crossing the river to the walkway leading to the other Dalmarnock House on Dalmarnock Greater estate.

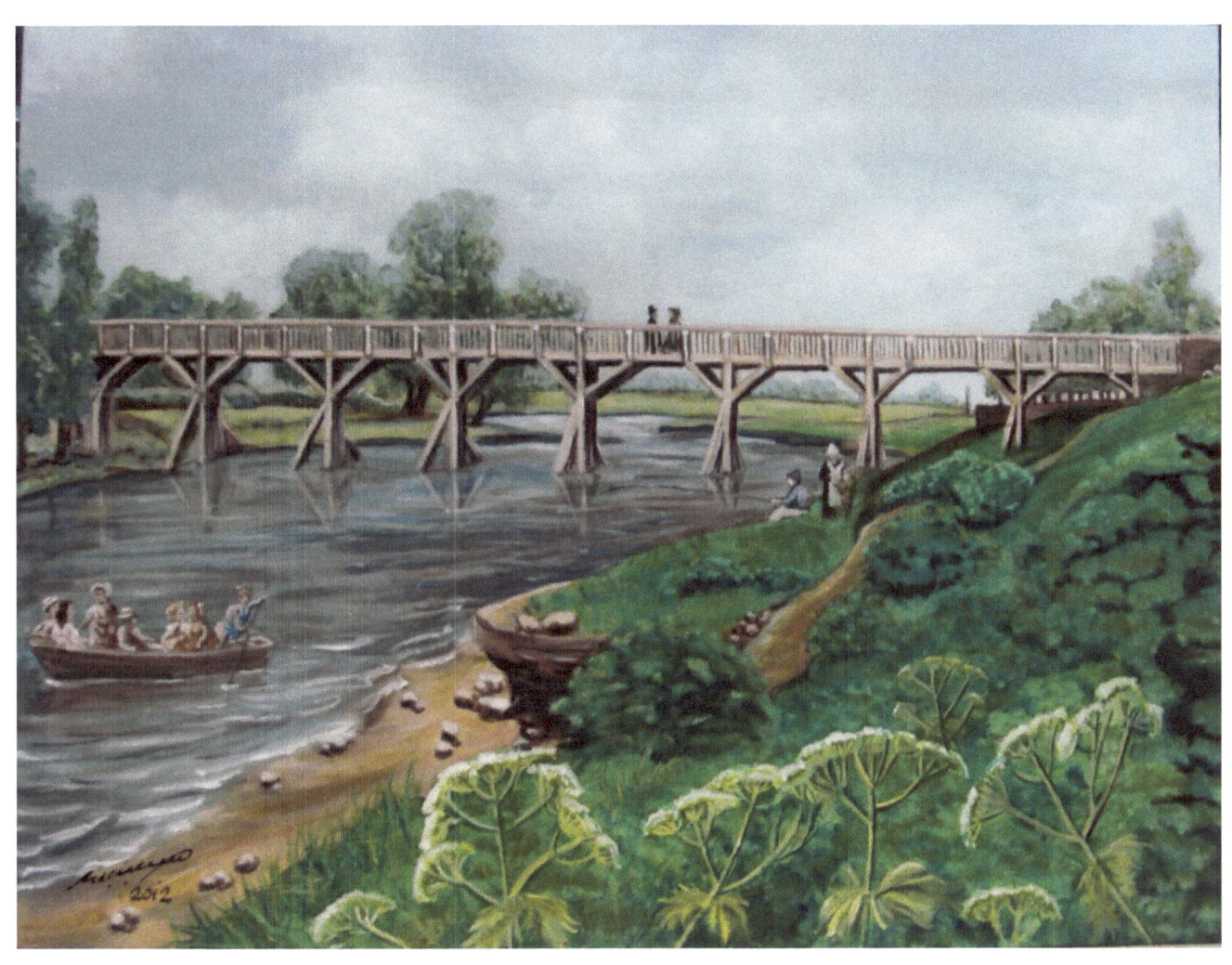

DALMARNOCK BRIDGE 1827 - © OCTOBER 2012
Acrylic on canvas board measuring 406 x 305 mm (16" x 12")

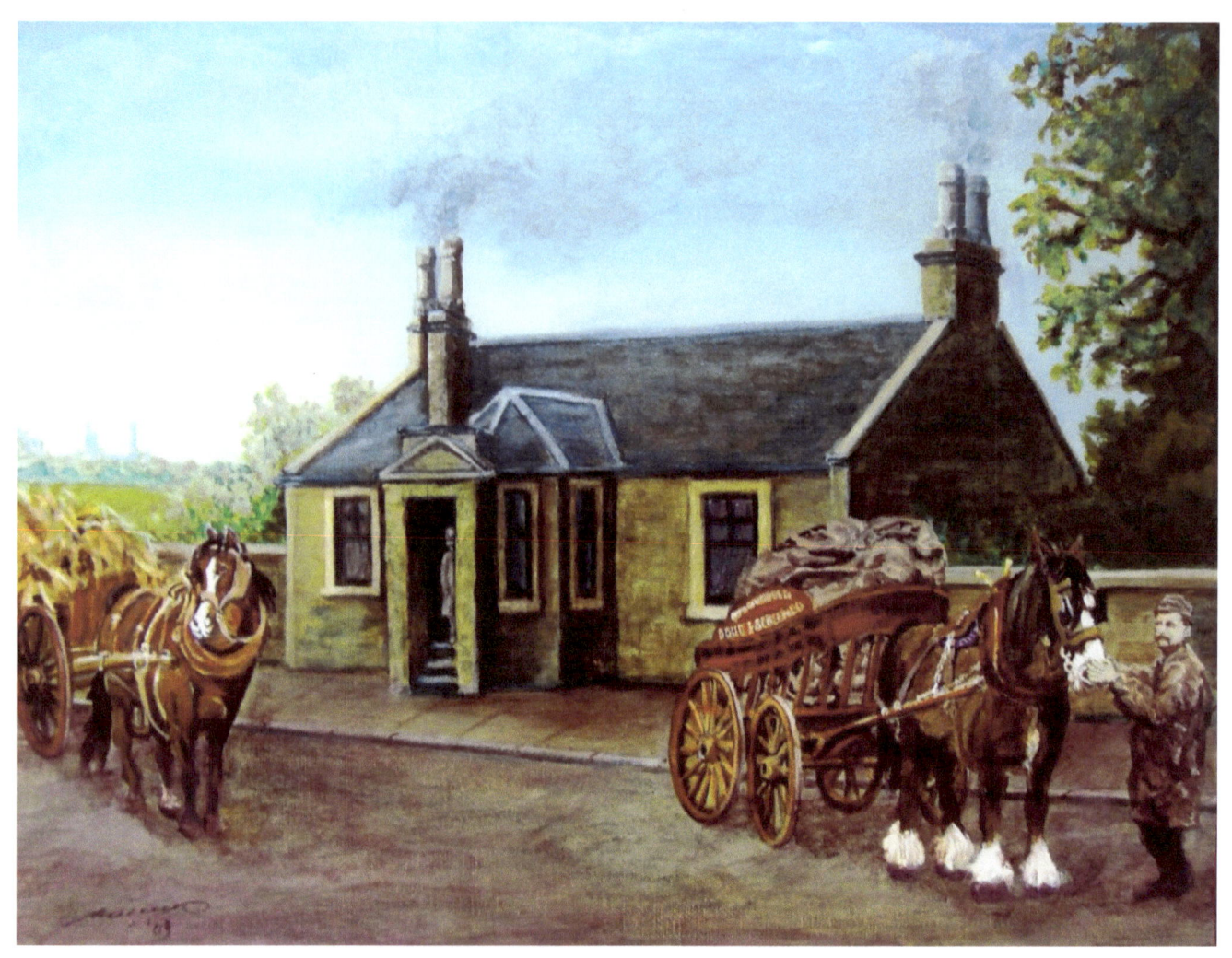

DALMARNOCK TOLLHOUSE - © SEPTEMBER 2009
Acrylic on canvas board measuring 406 x 305 mm (16" x 12")

How the tollhouse, may have looked in the early 19th century. Carters stop to pay their dues after crossing Dalmarnock Bridge from Rutherglen. The tollhouse, famous for its chimney above the front door, was later used by Glasgow Corporation Transport and then as commercial premises and as a doctor's surgery. The building was demolished in 2011 as part of the Clyde Gateway project.

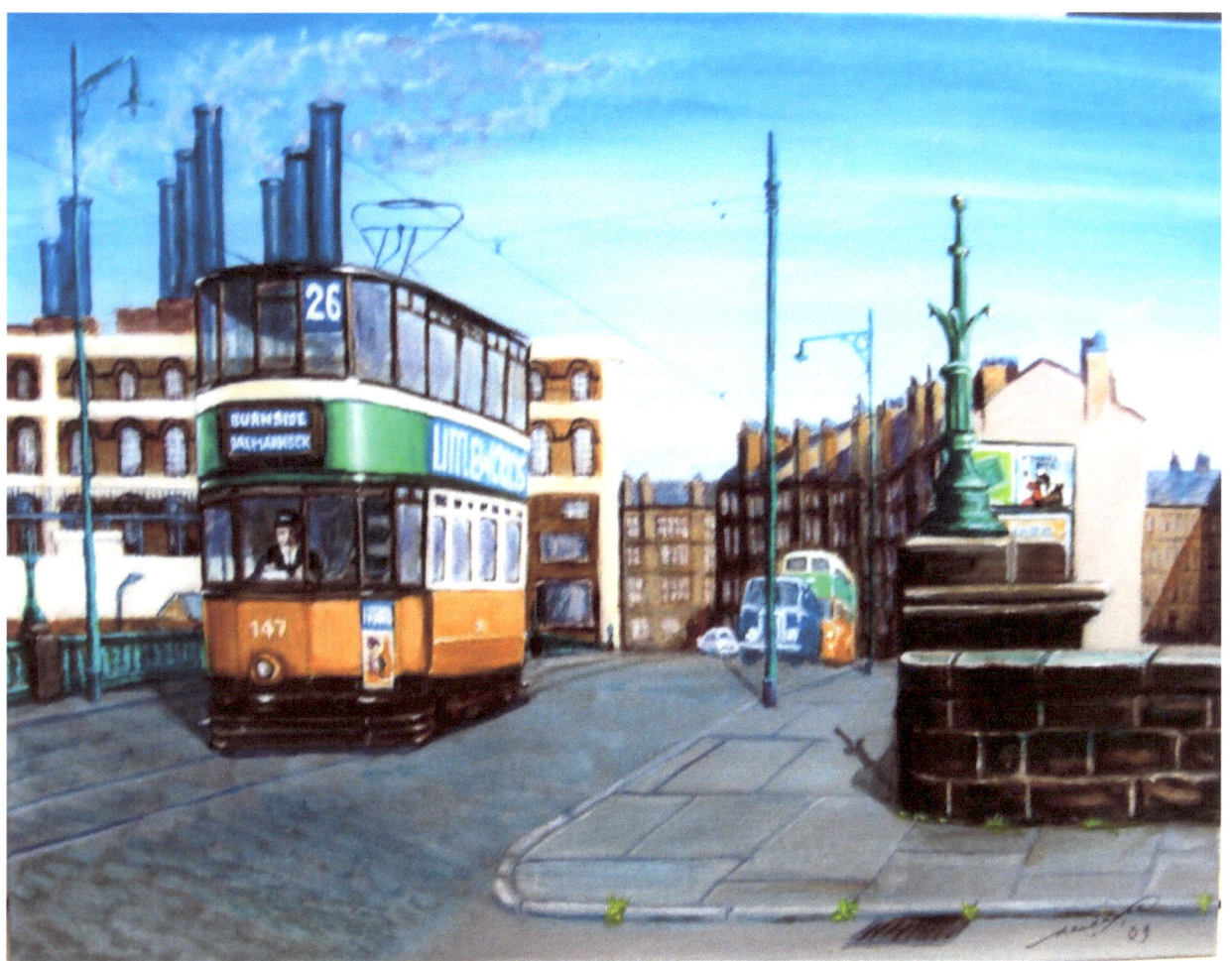

DALMARNOCK BRIDGE 1960 - © FEBRUARY 2009

Acrylic on canvas board measuring 406 x 305 mm (16" x 12")

Service number 26, standard hex-dash, tramcar crosses the bridge en route to Burnside. The view is from Downiebrae Road on the Rutherglen side of the bridge looking north. On the left is Dalmarnock Electric Power Station, built on the site of Dalmarnock House, and opposite the red sandstone tenements that survived bombing of the power station during World War II (1939-45) and which are still standing today. The Boundary Bar public house was located at the corner of Dalmarnock Road and Birkwood Street, the tenement building in the background.

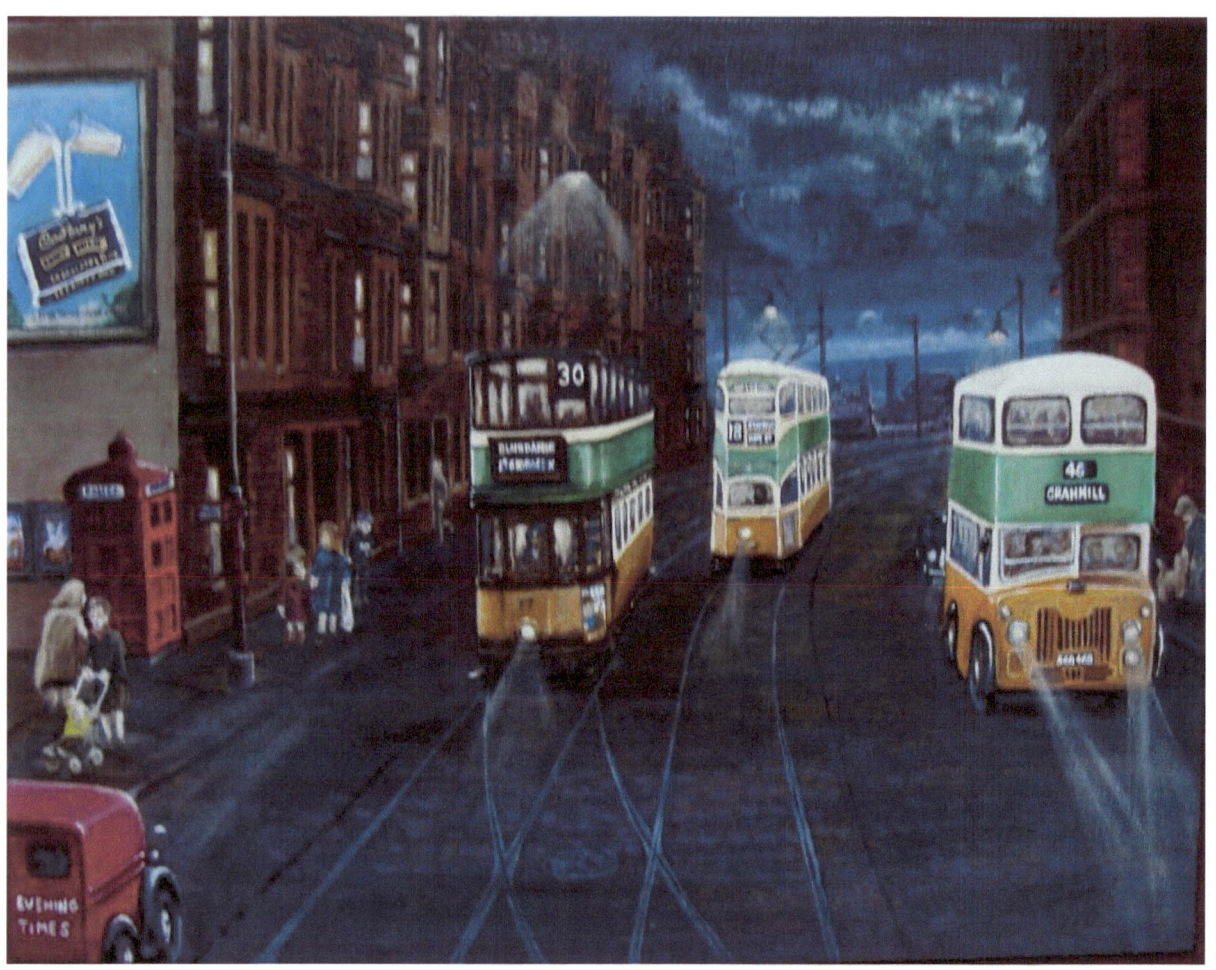

DALMARNOCK CROSSOVER AT BIRKWOOD STREET - © FEBRUARY 2011

Acrylic on canvas board measuring 406 x 305 mm (16" x 12")

Looking south Dalmarnock Bridge is in the background with Downiebrae Road factories. Dalmarnock Electric Power Station is the building to the right of service number 46 motor bus en route to Cranhill from Castlemilk. Service number 30 tramcar is about to use the crossover at its terminus at Birkwood Street, located immediately to the left of the *Evening Times* delivery van. It will then head to Blairdardie in the northwest of the city via Parkhead Cross and St George's Cross. Coronation Mark I tramcar, service number 18, is en route to Springburn from Burnside.

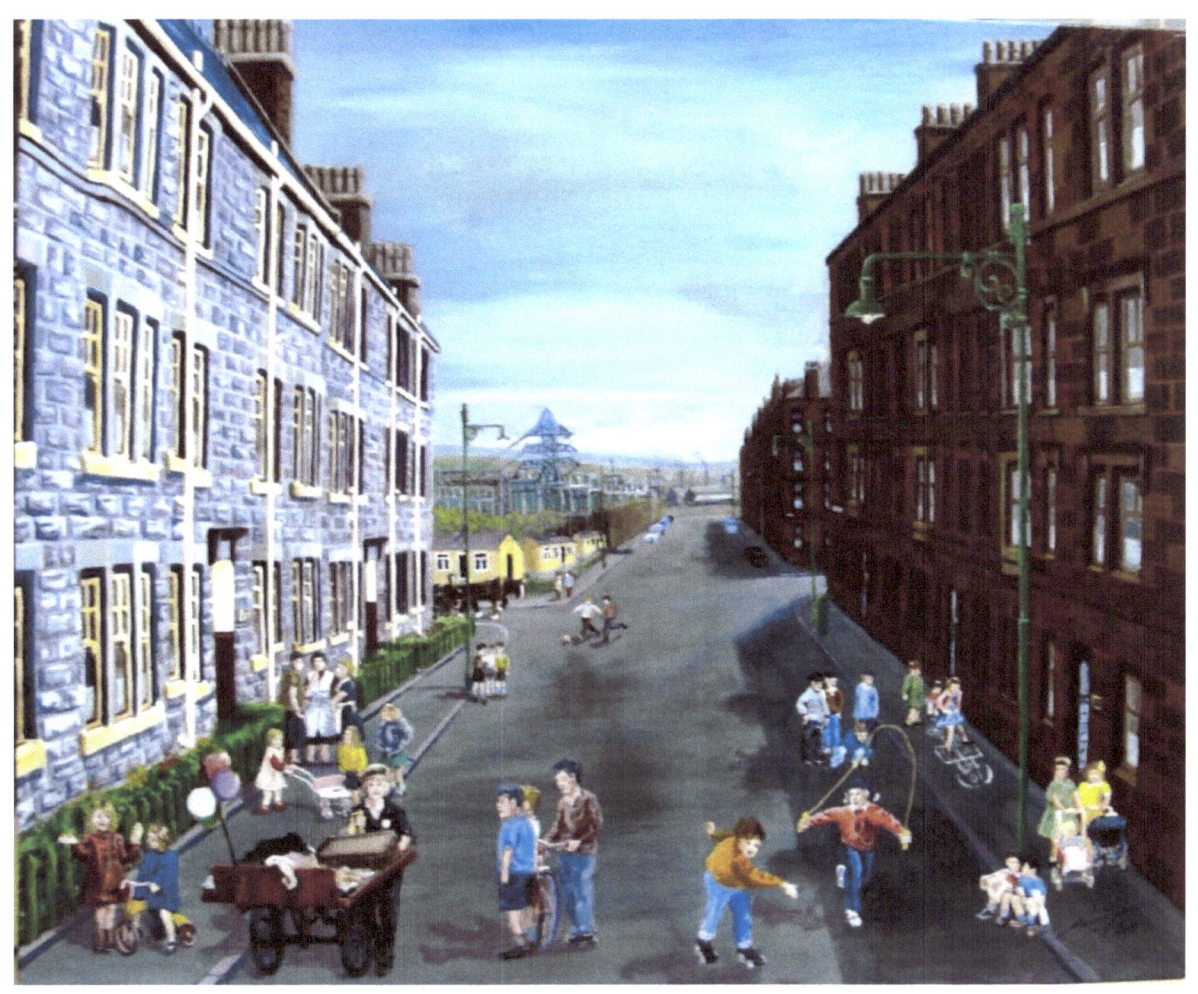

WODDROP STREET, DALMARNOCK - © MAY 2011
Acrylic on canvas board measuring 508 x 406 mm (20" x 16")

Woddrop Street runs parallel to Dalmarnock Road between Allan Street and the River Clyde at Dalmarnock Bridge. Dunclutha Street on the left leads to Dalmarnock Recreation Ground which had football pitches, bowling greens and tennis courts. Birkwood Street on the right leads to Dalmarnock Road. Looking south from Allan Street towards Rutherglen the painting shows the three types of housing available to residents at the end of World War II (1939 - 1945) and weans playing in the street around the 1950's.

DALMARNOCK RAILWAY STATION

On 24 June 1861 Glasgow Central Railway opened the Rutherglen to Dalmarnock goods and mineral line, including a bridge over the River Clyde about 325 yards (300 metres) southwest of Dalmarnock House.   A station named Bridgeton was built at the junction of Swanston Street and Dalmarnock Road. An embankment and iron bridge was constructed over Dalmarnock Road to carry goods and mineral traffic to London Road Station in 1877, Parkhead Forge, Rolling Mills and Steel Works in 1885 and beyond to Blochairn Junction in 1886. By 1891 Bridgeton Station was also serving passengers travelling on steam trains on the Glasgow Central low level line (tunnel) via Bridgeton Cross, Glasgow Green and Glasgow Cross stations. Bridgeton Station closed and a new station, renamed Dalmarnock Station, opened on 1 November 1895 when the Caledonian Railway Company introduced passenger services from Rutherglen to Dalmarnock. Dalmarnock Station closed to passengers on 5 October 1964. However a new Dalmarnock Station, with its entrance in Swanston Street, was opened in November 1979 to provide commuter services from Hamilton and Motherwell on the new Argyle line into Glasgow Central Station and beyond to the western suburbs.

The iron railway bridge over Dalmarnock Road was removed in June 2009 and Dalmarnock Station was temporarily closed on 4 June 2012 to enable removal of the embankment and a complete reconstruction of the station. The revamped station with its entrance and ticket office in Dalmarnock Road has lifts to its below street level platforms. The new multi-million pound Dalmarnock Station will play an important role when Glasgow hosts the 2014 Commonwealth Games because of its close proximity to the Athletes' Village and other venues.

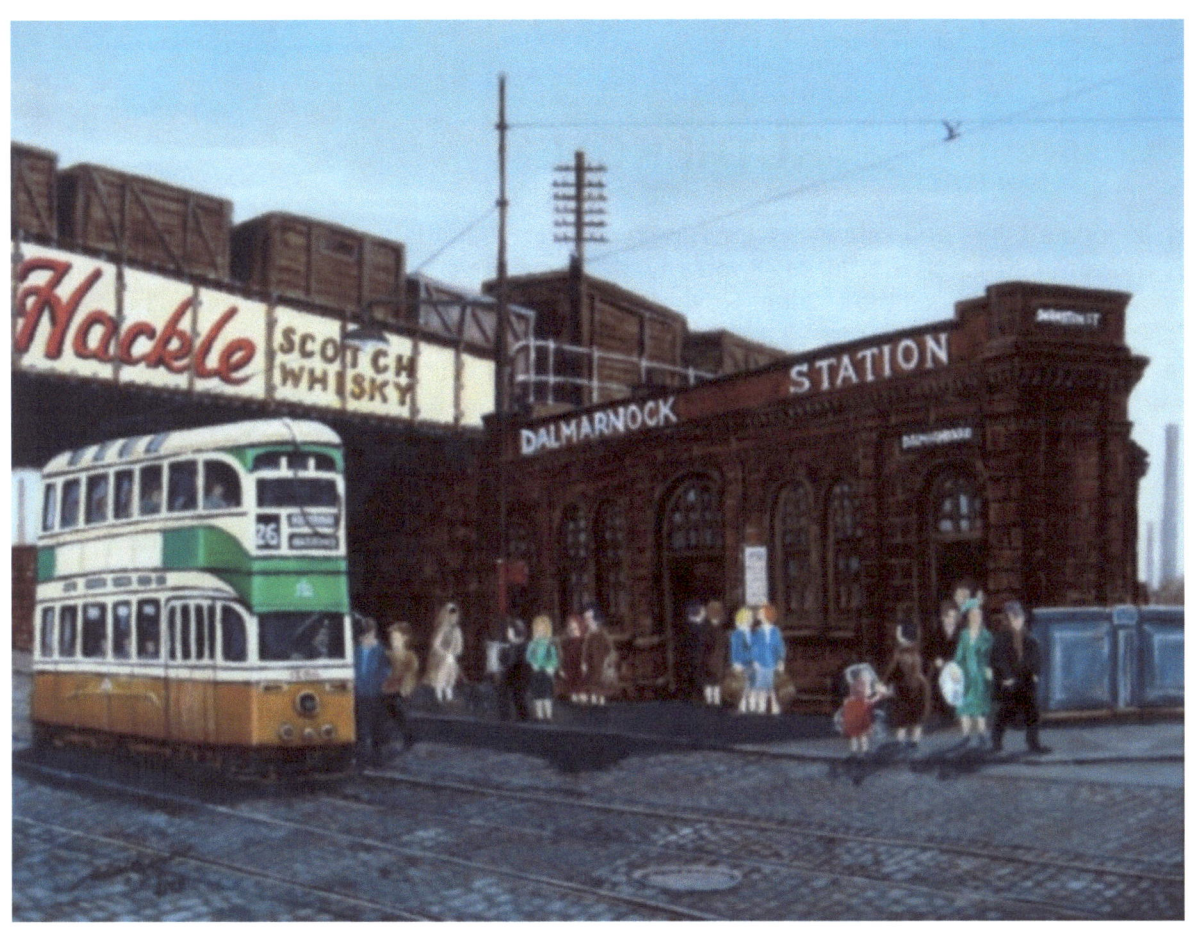

DALMARNOCK RAILWAY STATION - © FEBRUARY 2013
Acrylic on canvas board measuring 406 x 305 mm (16" x 12")

The frontage of Dalmarnock Railway Station as it was from its opening in 1895 until its closure in 1964. Coronation Mark I tram, service number 26, en route from Rutherglen to Scotstoun, passes beneath the iron bridge carrying goods traffic. All tram services in Glasgow were withdrawn by 4 September 1962 and the last of the regular steam trains were withdrawn on 29 April 1967.

RUTHERGLEN

Rutherglen is located in Lanarkshire on the south eastern boundary of Glasgow (Dalmarnock). Rutherglen was granted its charter in 1126, only two years after David I ascended to the throne of Scotland, making it one of Scotland's oldest Royal Burghs. The accolade helped make Rutherglen an important centre for trade. During the 19th century Rutherglen changed from a weaving and mining village to a more industrialised area with its own shipyard, established by Thomas Bollen Seath in 1856. Seath built many of the paddle steamers and the famous little Clutha ferry boats that transported commuters up and down the River Clyde. In the 19th century Rutherglen was also widely known for the many horse fairs which were held regularly in the town on its wide pavements and Main Street which still exist today. Rutherglen Town Hall, a famous local landmark, is a unique Scottish Baronial style building, originally constructed in 1862 with a 110ft (34 metre) clock tower. The grade A listed building has always played an important part in the history and local life of the community. Following a £12.5 million refurbishment, the Town Hall re-opened in early 2005 and is now a premier location for arts and cultural activities, exhibitions, conferencing, banqueting and weddings.

Glasgow Corporation's tramcar service number 18 served Rutherglen Main Street between 1938 and 1955. From Bridgeton Cross the service was routed along Main Street Bridgeton, Rutherglen Bridge, Shawfield, Main Street Rutherglen and Stonelaw Road where it either crossed over and headed back into the city to Springburn or carried on up Stonelaw Road to Burnside before crossing over and returning to Springburn. Service number 26 (Burnside or Rutherglen and Scotstoun, Clydebank or Dalmuir West) was introduced in 1943 to run via Dalmarnock Road, Farmeloan Road and Stonelaw Road. On 23 January 1949 the service to Rutherglen was extended via Main Street Rutherglen to Oatlands at Roseberry Street. On 7 August 1955 following the removal of trams from Main Street, Rutherglen, Burnside trams were diverted from Bridgeton Cross to run via Dalmarnock Road, Farmeloan Road and Stonelaw Road. The Rutherglen portion was curtailed at Shawfield and renumbered 18A and 26A. Electric trolleybus service number 101 (Riddrie and Rutherglen) via Glasgow Cross was introduced in 1956 and operated until 29 April 1966.

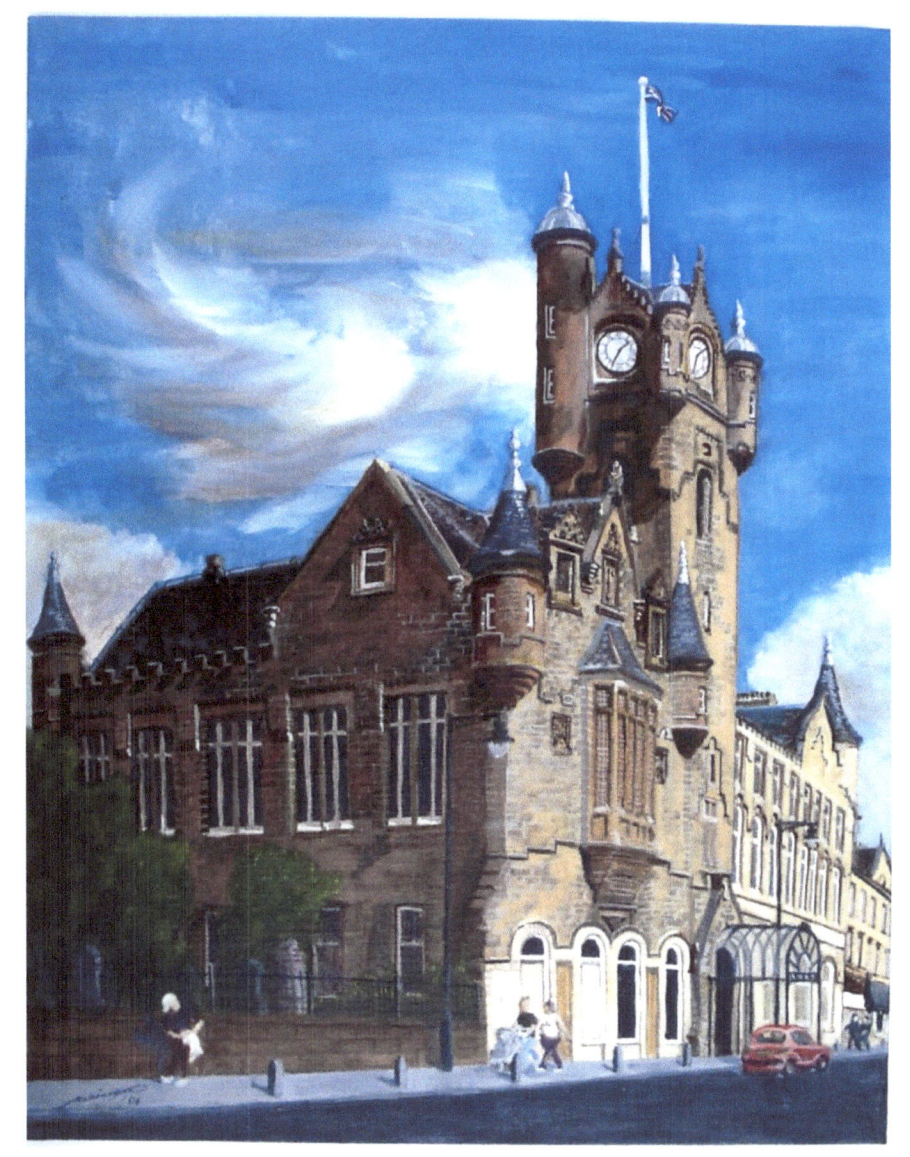

RUTHERGLEN TOWN HALL - © DECEMBER 2006

Acrylic on canvas board measuring 508 x 406 mm (20" x 16")

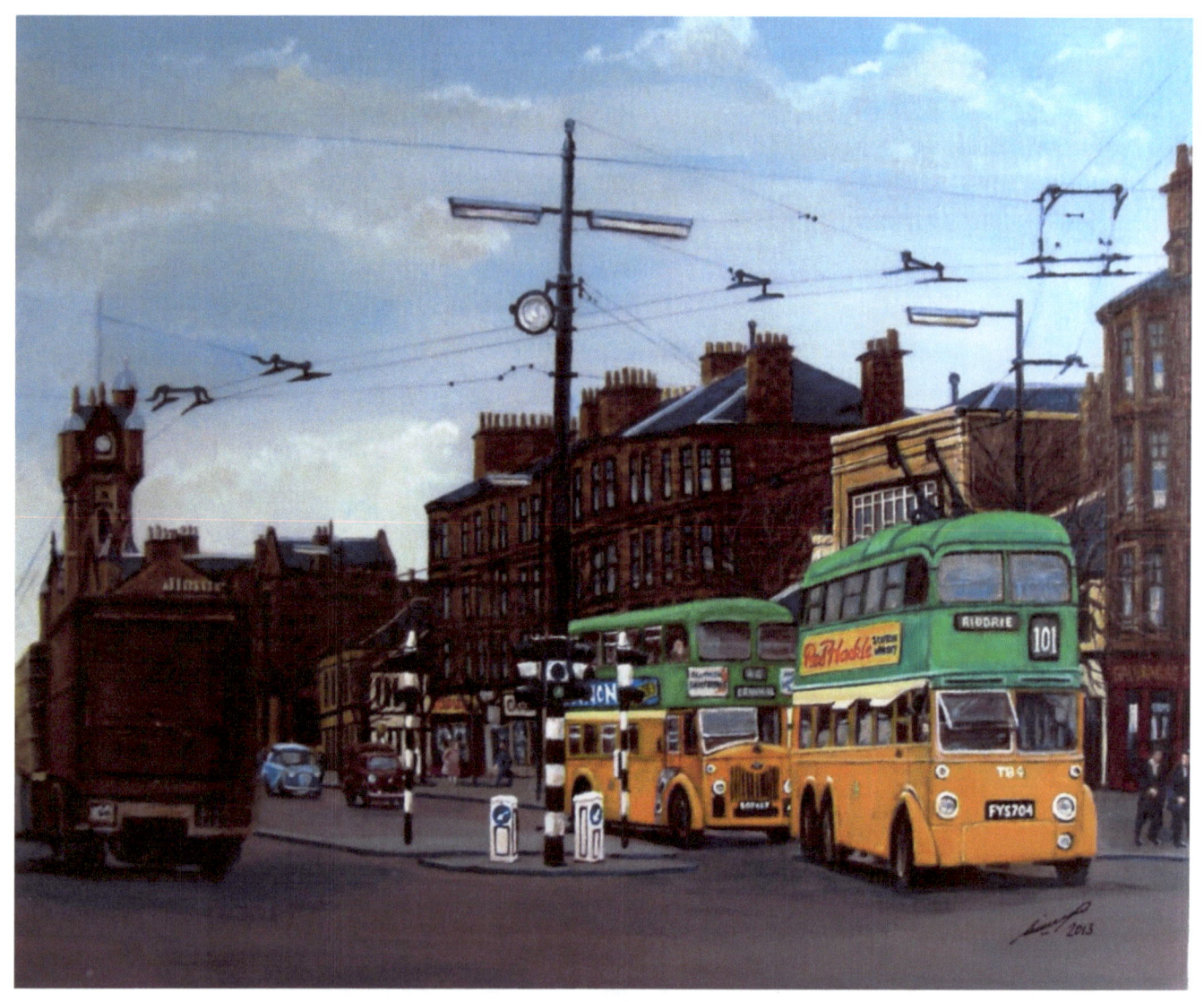

MAIN STREET RUTHERGLEN - © FEBRUARY 2013
Acrylic on canvas board measuring 508 x 406 mm (20" x 16")

A three-axle electric trolleybus, service 101 (Riddrie and Rutherglen), is about to negotiate the anti-clockwise terminal loop at the east end of Main Street on 29 April 1966, the final day of its service. It is followed by service number 46 motor bus en route to Cranhill from Castlemilk.

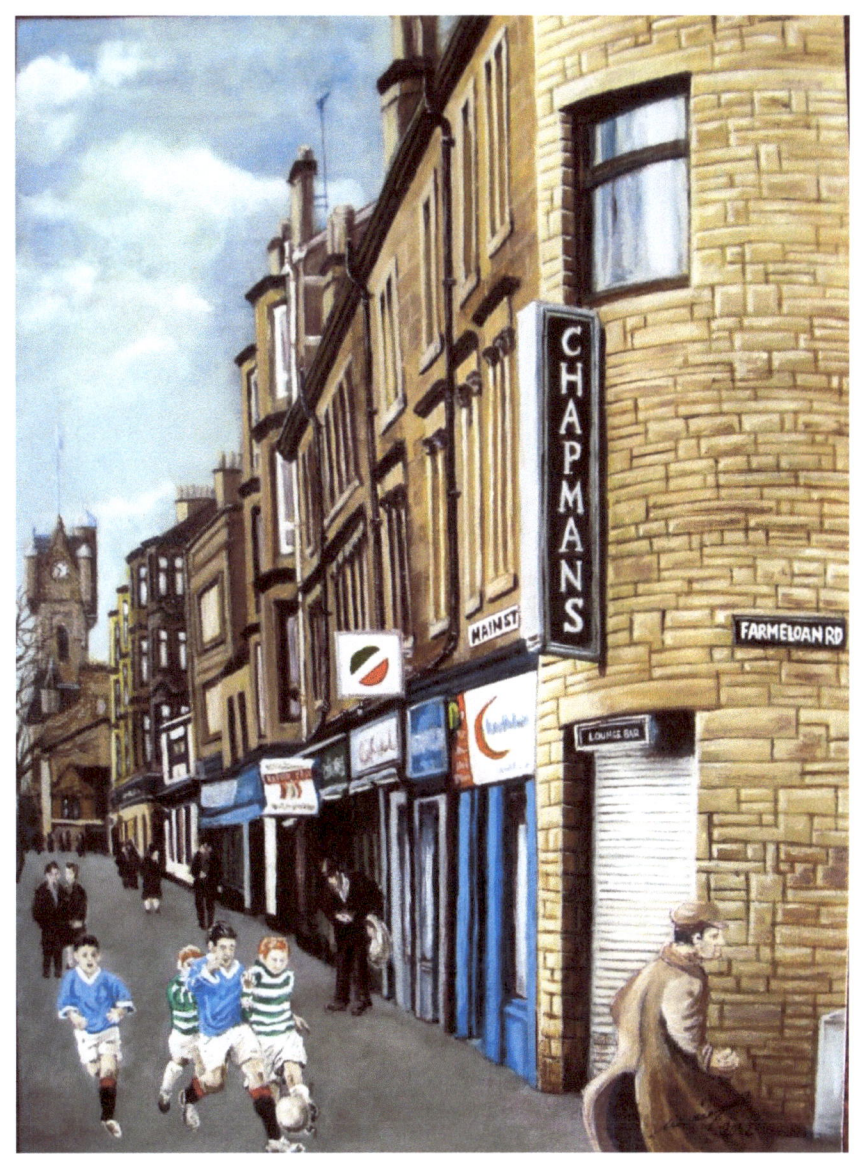

CHAPMANS CORNER, RUTHERGLEN - © FEBRUARY 2012
Acrylic on canvas board measuring 406 x 305 mm (16" x 12")

Chapmans, a long, narrow, public house is situated at the east end of Main Street at its junction with Farmeloan Road. The boys in their Rangers and Celtic strips kick a ball along the wide, tree-lined, pavement fronting the buildings in Main Street.

EXTRACTS FROM GLESCA PALS MESSAGE BOARD

scotyankee (Toronto, Ohio, USA) "…..glesca artist I tip my hat to you, your paintings are great and I like the wee bit of history that comes with them."

bettyb (Fergus, Ontario, Canada) "….absolutely fantastic glesca artist…just brilliant as usual".

Ronnie (London, England, UK) "…wonderful paintings glesca artist".

kathy (Calton, Glasgow, Scotland) " ….I jist love the two wee lassies playing peever u have captured the era to a 'T' and of course the pub my da worked in".

henrietta (Denmark, Europe) " ….I bought two original paintings by glesca artist …I love them"

Ella (Long Island, New York, USA) "….your paintings are just great. Thanks for sharing them with us".

joyce (Rutherglen, Scotland) "…wow what brill paintings. I just love them all….great work".

Wilmab (Hampshire, England, UK) "…I have enjoyed looking at your paintings. I especially like the black and white graphite sketches. Your drawing of the York Shambles is exactly as I remember it".

jimmyNZ (New Zealand) " ….your paintings are lovely."

Nell (London, England, UK) "…love them aw. Thanks for the memory".

Lizzy (Cambridge, England, UK) "…wonderful paintings…it just captures the image of Glasgow and its weans".

Beth (Durban, South Africa) "…these paintings are magnificent".

Liz (Renfrew, Scotland) "….what wonderful paintings. The one with the kids playing in the street brought back so many memories".

Visit Glesca Pals Message Board at:

www.glescapals.com